W9-COO-284

FORGIVE US OUR PRESS PASSES

SELECTED WORKS BY DANIEL SCHORR

A PUBLICATION IN CELEBRATION OF
THE TWENTIETH ANNIVERSARY OF THE
HASTINGS COMMUNICATIONS AND ENTERTAINMENT LAW JOURNAL
O'BRIEN CENTER FOR SCHOLARLY PUBLICATIONS
UNIVERSITY OF CALIFORNIA, HASTINGS COLLEGE OF THE LAW
SAN FRANCISCO

Edited by Matthew Passmore & Chip Robertson
Cover and book design by Matthew Passmore & David Schnider

Published by
The O'Brien Center for Scholarly Publications
University of California, Hastings College of the Law
San Francisco, California

Printed in the United States of America.
First printing, August 1998.
Second printing, January 1999.

Library of Congress Catalog Card No. 98-86519

ISBN 0-9626954-6-7
ISSN 1061-6578

HASTINGS COMMUNICATIONS
AND ENTERTAINMENT LAW JOURNAL

COMM/ENT

VOLUME 20   **1998**

CONTENTS

Editor's Preface

When the editors of the *Hastings Communications and Entertainment Law Journal* were searching for ways to properly commemorate our twentieth anniversary of publication, we hit upon the idea of asking various luminaries to submit brief tracts on legal issues they believed to be of current import. Toward this end, we faxed a request to Daniel Schorr to see if he would be willing to make a submission. To our surprise and gratification, Mr. Schorr faxed back a short piece entitled "Forgive Us Our Press Passes" the day after our initial request.

From this auspicious beginning grew the idea of publishing a collection of Mr. Schorr's papers, articles, and speeches to share with future generations of law and journalism students. These pieces span the past quarter-century of his illustrious career in both written and broadcast journalism: from the FBI investigation that would become part of the Articles of Impeachment of President Nixon, through the end of the Cold War and the prosecution of the Gulf War, to the progressive devolution of "the news" into sensationalistic entertainment. This collection also contains Mr. Schorr's reflections on the role of the media in society, the effects of television on the development of the journalistic craft, privacy and secrecy, the First Amendment, and government suppression of information. As such, we consider it an excellent and fitting celebration of our twentieth year.

Mr. Schorr is no stranger to COMM/ENT. In 1977, he participated in a roundtable discussion at the University of California, Berkeley entitled "What Are the Limitations on Freedom of the Press?" with Dean Sanford H. Kadish and Professor Jesse H. Choper, both of Berkeley's Boalt Hall School of Law. That discussion was published in the inaugural issue of COMM/ENT, and Mr. Schorr's comments are reprinted in this issue as well. In 1996 Mr. Schorr again traveled to the University of California, this time to Hastings College of the Law to deliver the Mathew O. Tobriner Memorial Lecture in honor of the late Justice Tobriner of California Supreme Court, who was also a Professor of Law at Hastings. This lecture, entitled "The First Amendment Under Pressure," was first published in Volume 18 of COMM/ENT and is also reprinted in this edition.

To preserve Mr. Schorr's unique voice, we minimized our editing of the pieces in this issue. However, wherever possible, we provided source references for quoted language and references to books and other publications, to increase the value of this collection as a research and teaching tool, as well as a chronicle of history.

We wish to thank William Safire, William Schneider, and Geoffrey Cowan for their warm and thoughtful introductions, Guy Raz at National Public Radio, Sandy Gilmelis at CBS, Ann Rubin at the *New York Times*, Hope Warschaw, Jean Campbell at the University of Southern California, Annenberg School for Communication, Albert Kaba at Hastings College of the Law, O'Brien Center for Scholarly Publications, the editorial board and staff of COMM/ENT (without whom this edition would never have come to fruition); and especially Daniel Schorr, for allowing us to pay this small tribute to his extraordinary career.

Matthew Passmore
Editor in Chief

Chip Robertson
Senior Articles Editor

University of California
Hastings College of the Law
San Francisco
June 1998

Biography of Daniel Schorr[†]

For more than half a century, Daniel Schorr has entered American homes to teach, challenge and enlighten us to the meaning of world events.

In 1946, Mr. Schorr began his career as a foreign correspondent, writing from postwar Europe for the *Christian Science Monitor* and later the *New York Times*. During this time he documented the effects of the Marshall Plan and the creation of the NATO alliance. In 1953, Mr. Schorr's vivid coverage of a disastrous flood that broke the dikes of the Netherlands caught the ear of Edward R. Murrow, the guiding spirit of CBS News, and Mr. Schorr joined CBS News as the diplomatic correspondent in Washington.

In 1955, Mr. Schorr opened the first post-Stalin CBS bureau in the Soviet Union. His two-and-a-half-year stay included the first-ever exclusive television interview with a Soviet leader, Nikita Khrushchev, which was filmed in Krushchev's Kremlin office in 1957 for CBS's *Face the Nation*. However, Mr. Schorr's repeated defiance of Soviet censorship eventually landed him in trouble with the KGB. After a brief arrest on trumped-up charges, he was barred from the Soviet Union at the end of 1957.

Returning to Washington in 1966, Mr. Schorr hung up his foreign correspondent's trenchcoat and settled down to "become re-Americanized," as he puts it, by plunging into coverage of civil rights, urban crisis and environmental problems.

In 1972, the Watergate break-in brought Mr. Schorr a full-time assignment as CBS's chief Watergate correspondent. His exclusive reports and on-the-scene coverage at the Senate Watergate hearings earned him three Emmy awards. Mr. Schorr unexpectedly found himself a part of his own story when the hearings turned up President Nixon's "enemies list" with his name on it and evidence that the president had ordered him investigated by the FBI. This "abuse of a federal agency" figured as one count in the Bill of Impeachment on which Nixon would have been tried had he not resigned in August, 1974. That fall, Mr. Schorr moved to cover investigations of CIA and FBI scandals—what he called "the son of Watergate." Once again, he

---

† This biography is adapted from the Biography of Daniel Schorr, available at <http://www.npr.org/inside/bios/dschorr.html> (visited Feb. 27, 1998).

became a part of his own story. In February 1976, when the House of Representatives voted to suppress the final report of its Intelligence Investigating Committee, Mr. Schorr arranged for publication of an advance copy he had exclusively obtained. This led to his suspension by CBS and an investigation by the House Ethics Committee in which Mr. Schorr was threatened with jail for contempt of Congress if he did not disclose his source. At a public hearing, he refused on First Amendment grounds, saying that "to betray a source would mean to dry up many future sources for many future reporters . . . It would mean betraying myself, my career and my life."

Mr. Schorr's half-century career has earned him many awards for journalistic excellence, including three television Emmys and decorations from the Queen of the Netherlands and the President of the Federal Republic of Germany. He also has been honored by civil liberties groups and professional organizations for his unwavering defense of the First Amendment. In 1995 he received a Gold Baton from the Alfred I. duPont-Columbia University organization to honor his "exceptional contributions to radio and television reporting and commentary." The most prestigious award in the field of broadcasting, the duPont-Columbia Gold Baton is considered the equivalent of the Pulitzer Prize in the field. Mr. Schorr also won the coveted Peabody Award in 1993 "for a lifetime of uncompromising reporting of the highest integrity" and the George Polk Radio Commentary Award for his interpretations of national and international events. He has also been inducted into the Hall of Fame of the Society of Professional Journalists.

Mr. Schorr currently interprets the news as Senior News Analyst for National Public Radio.

Daniel Schorr

Photo by Marvin Jones

A Prolegomenon

by
WILLIAM SAFIRE*

"I cannot betray a news source."

So many of us in journalism have said or written that. On occasion, I have embellished that flat statement to reassure a source that what it (I use *it* to disguise the source's sex) tells me will be used in a way that will not reveal its identity: "I am prepared to go to jail," I say dramatically, "or better still, to see my publisher go to jail, rather than subvert the First Amendment by exposing my source to retribution." But as we wrap ourselves in our constitutional protections (which are not ironclad when they conflict with fair-trial rights) few reporters are faced with the immediate prospect of actual punishment.

Dan Schorr was. An angry Congressional committee came this close—I am holding my index finger a quarter inch from my thumb—to citing him for contempt. Some of our Representatives were ready to throw him in the cooler for publishing a document they wanted suppressed, and for refusing to reveal the name of the person who "leaked" it to him.

Schorr did not strike a defiant pose; he is not the sort who longs for well-publicized martyrdom. On the contrary, he was most respectful in his refusal, but held firm, and was supported by his network's gusty lawyer, Joe Califano. To betray a source, he told the Congress, "would mean betraying myself, my career and my life." As a result, the Ethics Committee wisely backed away from the harassment of a man who had demonstrated to the public his ingrained code of ethics.

That was typical of the Schorr mode of operation: to cover coolly, to comment judiciously, to convey excitement unexcitedly—but to follow the story where it leads and not to shy away from controversy. The Schorr approach is to grab the viewer or listener by the intellect rather than by the lapels.

---

* Author and former speechwriter for President Richard M. Nixon, Mr. Safire currently writes for the *New York Times*.

1

One reason for that gently tough-minded approach is that he was present at the creation of what Eric Severeid called "electronic journalism." Dan is the last of Edward R. Murrow's band of correspondents to remain in the trenches. The last of these CBS Mohicans carries on not only its tradition of integrity but brings along an institutional memory.

Schorr knew Senator Joe McCarthy before he was an "ism." He remembers the "spirit of Geneva" even though the players in that Khruchchev-Eisenhower summit have long since become spirits themselves. He carries in his head a file of the arcane maneuverings of the world of espionage when all other files have been expunged or shredded or conveniently forgotten. And few of the horde of reporters covering present-day political scandals can match the Schorr "gate" credentials: his coverage of the Watergate scandal earned him a revered place on the reportorial hall of fame known as President Nixon's "enemies list." (Dan and I met when I was a Nixon speechwriter; even so, we became friends. We come at things with a different ideological mindset, but find ourselves in agreement on the big things.)

He draws on his half-century in journalism to inform his commentaries on National Public Radio, where he serves as Senior News Analyst. He still works the phones and plumbs his sources to get to the nub of an issue, but he is able to do a stakeout on his own mind: at long last, Dan has reached the point where he can leak to himself.

That makes him not just a source to his colleagues to be mined and protected, but a resource to be cherished by audiences who hear him on the air and who attend his lectures at universities across the country. In those carefully written talks, he has more time to delve into the workings of our profession and to discuss the conflicts between secrecy and freedom, between government-media symbiosis and manipulation. The *Hastings Communications and Entertainment Law Journal* at the University of California, Hastings College of the Law has done a service to the law, to journalism and to history in tracking down and bookifying some of the best examples of the Schorr thinking over the past generation.

Some journalists are pure observers, reporting events from afar with a fine detachment. Others, whether they seek it or not, become participants in the events they cover. When that happens, the observer-participant faces the challenge of seeing the story from more than one side. Very few can examine their own motives and comment on their own actions with the same objectivity as they afford other participants. When placed in that professional pickle, Schorr has never been an apologist, even for himself; that's what makes him unique among analysts.

It's part of the persnickety integrity that always drives his coverage and used to drive some of his network bosses up the wall. Listen to his voice as you read these speeches and papers. In his written words, you can hear the cadences of the oral communicator— the understandable argument, the illuminating anecdote, the familiar style. And underneath that, the editorial voice of one of the few great broadcast journalists of our time—scrupulously honest, historically fair, fearlessly forthright, and sometimes even deliciously insightful.

Introduction

by
WILLIAM SCHNEIDER[*]

Daniel Schorr is in danger of becoming a personality.

It is a danger he knows all too well, having spent his life in the broadcasting industry. "There is a special American fascination with personalities recognized from the Tube," Schorr said in his Aspen Institute lecture in 1976. And he abhors it.

As Schorr points out in these pages, it is not just the press that is ruled by personality. It is also government. "Spin patrol, damage control, message of the day . . . the process has become so ingrained as to make governing seem like a form of theatre," he said in his Theodore H. White Memorial Lecture at Harvard University in 1993.

Where personality rules, the truth often becomes a casualty. Truth becomes relative. It becomes Ronald Reagan's truth or Bill Clinton's truth, sold by the force of their distinctive personalities. Or a dramatized version of the truth sold by the press to give the story more "personality." In his "Confessions of a Journalist at Age 75," Schorr warns us that "the fabric of television is a fabric of small deceptions."

Daniel Schorr has devoted his career to the service of the truth—as an author, columnist and teacher, and most prominently as a broadcaster for twenty-five years with CBS News, six years at CNN and most recently at National Public Radio. He is renowned for taking on big government in the service of the truth, often at considerable peril to himself. Schorr has been called an "enemy" of the Nixon White House, of the CIA, the FBI and the House of Representatives Ethics Committee. But never, ever, an enemy of the people.

Schorr has been equally fearless in taking on the power of big media, including his own employers, also at considerable peril to himself. He recounts in these pages how big media is often as abusive and manipulative as big government. "People used to admire the 'power press,' a force for exposure of evil," he told the audience of the School of Journalism commencement at Berkeley in 1990. Now "[t]hey

---

[*] Senior Political Analyst, Cable News Network.

are as likely to resent the 'power of the media,' regarded as a force for manipulation."

Schorr says he has "the reporter's ethic"—"I cannot stand in the way of information getting to the public." But sometimes he does, and he recounts the agonizing conflicts every reporter is familiar with: when he or she has to choose between reporting the truth and withholding information in service to another valid objective.

Good journalism is not about rule-making. It's about risk-taking. Specifically, taking risks for the truth: the risk of being condemned by the government, the risk of antagonizing your employers and even the risk of telling people what they don't want to know.

Daniel Schorr understands those risks. He has taken them. And he wants us to regard such risk-taking, not as the calling of a unique personality, but as an essential requirement for the practice of journalism.

Introduction

by
GEOFFREY COWAN[*]

For more than forty years, the name Daniel Schorr has been synonymous with the best in journalism. From his years at CBS through his years at National Public Radio, he continues to inspire as well as educate all who know or hear him. Several of the essays in this volume derive from or refer to his visit to the University of California Berkeley as a Regents Professor in 1977, shortly after he left CBS. Part of that time was spent at UCLA where I, as a member of the Communications Studies faculty, was privileged to attend his lectures. They were filled with anecdotes and insights that I have quoted ever since. For example, he described the caption on pictures showing President Gerald Ford at his desk "studying" for his debate with Jimmy Carter. Ford wasn't studying at all, Schorr pointed out. He was posing for the cameras. Indeed, it was possibly the one time during the afternoon when he *wasn't* studying. Then he described his live CBS TV interview with a man in a bar in the Netherlands moments after Neil Armstrong's craft landed on the moon. "What did you think of that?" Schorr asked. "I liked it better the first time," answered the man at the bar. He wasn't drunk. He watched a simulation on television before the actual landing. In the incredible mix of technological marvels, of space landings and satellite photos from the moon, he had not been able to distinguish simulation from reality.

When Schorr visited UCLA and Berkeley in 1977, National Public Radio was only a speck on the horizon. In the two decades since then, NPR has become one of the nation's premier sources of news and information, and it has become a second, and even better, home for Schorr's talents. Some of his colleagues at NPR, most notably Cokie Roberts, have gone on to fame as television journalists. But Schorr has thrived at NPR, which has given him the luxury to explore serious issues in depth, to provide the context for great events, to engage in thoughtful exchanges with his colleagues, and to know that

---

[*] Dean, Annenberg School for Communication, University of Southern California.

his work was appreciated by a large, genuinely interested audience, and by the management of public radio. His voice—not just the timbre of his voice, but his distinctive "voice" as a writer—works particularly well on radio, which, at its best, engages our minds rather than our emotions. Deep in my memory, I can recall the voice of great radio commentators such as Elmer Davis, but theirs was a breed that faded and seemed to die with the advent of television. Appearances were deceiving. For the past two decades we have had Daniel Schorr, radio's Walter Lippman.

During the decades since his visit to UCLA, I have been privileged to get to know Dan Schorr as a friend and mentor. Of the countless moments we have shared, I remember particularly the wellspring of emotion at his eightieth birthday party, where he was surrounded by the thoughtful and the powerful, by the journalists and decision-makers who have profited from his wisdom. One picture that comes to mind as this is written, in the week after Fred Friendly's death, is of Dan and Fred, two men who invented radio and television journalism, who carried on the tradition of Edward R. Murrow, and who never lost faith in the Constitution and in the responsibility and the power of the press.

This collection provides all of us with a wonderful opportunity to spend a few quiet and thoughtful evenings alone with Daniel Schorr.

Forgive Us Our Press Passes[†]

Indulge me, at eighty-one, in some curmudgeonly ruminations about the journalistic craft I have loved, not always wisely, but well.

We are in trouble. It is the natural order of things that we be in trouble with the powerful, whom we try to monitor. But today we are in trouble with the powerless, who identify us more with the powerful than with them. And people are no longer willing to forgive us our press passes.

Press-bashing has become a growth industry, joined in by some of our colleagues. James Fallows, editor of *U.S. News and World Report*, has a book accusing us of undermining American democracy for fun and profit.[1] Howard Kurtz of the *Washington Post* says we have become our own worst enemy.[2] Ellen Hume says that American life is in trouble and journalists who could help are doing more harm than good.[3]

What is a journalist today anyway? A blow-dried television personality trained to read a teleprompter? A talk show host spreading conspiracy and hate? A George Stephanopoulos, who has gone through the revolving door to be paid by ABC for saying what he used to say on the White House payroll? A Pat Buchanan, who keeps body and hope alive between campaigns for President by selling celebrityhood on CNN?

Oh for the day of Ed Murrow, invited in his declining CBS days to run for Senator in New York and tempted to do so—until he concluded that, if he did, he would confuse his audience, left to wonder whether his past commentaries had been colored by his future political plans. How many television stars today, between entertaining appearances on TV and lucrative lecture dates in person, think of obligation to the people out there, now called the market?

---

†. This article was originally published under the same title in the *Hastings Communications and Entertainment Law Journal* at 20 HASTINGS COMM/ENT L.J. 269 (1998).

1. *See* JAMES FALLOWS, BREAKING THE NEWS: HOW THE MEDIA UNDERMINE AMERICAN DEMOCRACY FOR FUN AND PROFIT (1996).

2. *See* Alexandra Marks, *After Years of Being Bashed, Media Start to Bash Themselves,* CHRISTIAN SCI. MONITOR, Jan. 30, 1996, at 1 (quoting Howard Kurtz).

3. *See* Ellen Hume, Book Review, COLUM. JOURN. REV., Mar. 13, 1996, at 49.

You would surely not expect me to spend more than three minutes without mentioning Richard Nixon. On February 23, 1973, speaking to John Dean, his words preserved on tape for posterity, President Nixon said, "Well, one helluva lot of people don't give one damn about the issue of the suppression of the press, etc." (On another segment of that tape, he referred to me as "that son-of-a-bitch," but let me not digress.) Nixon was a good reader of the popular mood. He had sent Vice President Spiro Agnew out to make a speech denouncing the "nattering nabobs of negativism" in the media, calling down on the networks of thousands of supporting letters and phone calls.

Since then, anti-media sentiment has grown by leaps and bounds. In a recent Roper-Freedom Forum-Parade poll,[4] fewer than twenty percent rated the ethics of journalists as high.[5] More alarming, sixty-five percent of respondents said there are times when publication or broadcast should be prevented.[6] Prevented? That is prior restraint we are talking about, advance censorship, the heart of the First Amendment. Did we win that fight in the Pentagon Papers case in the Supreme Court[7] only now to lose it in the court of public opinion?

That is a serious matter. The practice of journalism rests on something called "privilege." Privilege is a special protection that society grants to some group because it serves society's purpose. We all have privilege against self incrimination. Doctors, lawyers, and the clergy have a special privilege to preserve confidentiality. And the First Amendment press privilege is the only privilege written into our Constitution to protect a single industry.

But the privilege accorded to the press depends on public support and will wither without it. The public today senses an abuse of privilege for profit and self-aggrandizement when Richard Jewell is falsely named as the prime suspect in the Atlanta bombing case.[8] Or when a Los Angeles television reporter falsely reports DNA findings in the O.J. Simpson case.[9] Or when a Dallas newspaper reports a

---

4. ROPER CENTER FOR PUBLIC OPINION RESEARCH, NEWS JUNKIES, NEWS CRITICS, HOW AMERICANS USE THE NEWS AND WHAT THEY THINK ABOUT IT (Feb. 1997) (on file with the *Hastings Communications and Entertainment Law Journal*) [hereinafter ROPER POLL].

5. *Id.* at 8.

6. *Id.* at 9.

7. *See* New York Times, Co. v. United States, 403 U.S. 713 (1971) (per curiam).

8. *See, e.g., Jewell Asks for Probe of Treatment by FBI Hearing,* L.A. TIMES, July 31, 1997, at A23.

9. *See, e.g.,* Howard Kurtz, *Bloody Sock Report Said to be "Incorrect,"* WASH. POST,

purported confession in the Oklahoma City bombing, which turns out to be a hoax.[10]

In all these cases the news organizations said they relied on confidential sources—and then invoked First Amendment protection against having to reveal those sources. But when a news organization relies on sources it cannot name, then it makes itself responsible for the accuracy of the story. So you had better think twice about how good your sources are. I say this as one who has occasionally been burned myself.

The *Washington Post*'s style book says we should always assume that information provided by confidential sources is weaker than information attributable to real people.[11] Not necessarily. Real people can lie and dissemble. Some informants, whistle-blowers with important stories to tell, must remain anonymous. Check out the information. But remember that when your confidential source has manipulated you, you do not get to justify yourself by saying you were had by someone you cannot name.

My concern is what we do to ordinary people and to the workings of justice. I am much more worried about the Richard Jewells than about government secrets. When it comes to the government and its millions of pages of mindlessly classified material, I have no doubt that this nation has suffered much more from undue secrecy than from undue disclosure. The government takes good care of itself. But protecting the ordinary citizen from defamation and invasion of privacy becomes our responsibility, and the public will judge us by how we carry out that responsibility.

I join in the general dismay of the journalistic community about the judgment against ABC for the methods used in its investigation of tainted food being sold by a Food Lion store.[12] ABC was using modern video techniques to do what Upton Sinclair was applauded for doing in penetrating a meat-packing plant in Chicago at the turn of the century.[13] His exposé led to the creation of the Food and Drug Administration.

Sept. 27, 1994, at A12.

10. *See* G. Robert Hillman, *News Denies Defense's Allegation That It Stole McVeigh Documents*, DALLAS MORNING NEWS, Mar. 4, 1997, at 1.

11. *See* Ben Bradley, *Standards and Ethics, in* WASHINGTON POST DESK BOOK ON STYLE (1984).

12. *See* Food Lion, Inc. v. Capitol Cities/ABC, Inc., 887 F. Supp. 811 (M.D.N.C. 1995).

13. *See* UPTON SINCLAIR, THE JUNGLE (1906).

So why was Sinclair applauded while ABC was slapped with a penalty of $5.5 million, which, perhaps coincidentally, is roughly what anchor Diane Sawyer earns annually?[14] Perhaps coincidentally, I say. But given the presence of a star who was not really a part of the investigation, given the concentration on video techniques and entertainment values in the remorseless quest of ratings, people can be forgiven if they no longer accept us as dedicated solely to the public weal, even when we perform a public service.

So where are we? Let's go back to that Roper poll. Eighty-two percent of respondents think reporters are insensitive to people's pain when covering disasters.[15] Sixty-four percent think the news is too sensationalized.[16] Sixty-three percent think the news is manipulated by special interests.[17] Fifty-eight percent think reporters too often quote confidential sources.[18]

I guess we have nowhere to go from here but up. But we have some trail markers for the way up. Young television reporters: Do not poke a microphone in the face of the person on the stretcher and ask, "How did it feel when the plane came down?" Young investigative reporter: Be careful of the friendly but nameless official who has a scoop for you that undermines somebody else's program. Police reporter: Watch out for the law enforcement officer who has a tip on the real guilty person. Producers: Do not regard people as "generic footage."

And to the great media organizations that employ these journalists: You are going to have to convince the public all over again that you are on its side. The *New York Times* and *Washington Post* made a good start on that when, contrary to rules and traditions, they agreed to publish the tract of the Unabomber under threat of further murders.[19] Serendipitously, that publication led to his being identified.

But more and more we will be under challenge to show whether we consider the public merely a market or part of a community in

---

14. *See* Howard Kurtz & Sue Ann Pressley, *Jury Finds Against ABC for $5.5 Million*, WASH. POST, Jan. 23, 1997, at A1. In August 1997, a federal judge reduced the punitive damages award to $315,000. *See* Lawrie Mifflin, *Judge Slashes $5.5 Million Award to Grocery Chain for ABC Report*, N.Y. TIMES, Aug. 30, 1997, at A1.

15. ROPER POLL, *supra* note 4, at 6.

16. *Id.* at 7.

17. *Id.*

18. *Id.* at 6.

19. *See* Howard Kurtz, *Unabomber Manuscript is Published*, WASH. POST, Sept. 19, 1995, at A1.

which we are joined. I would like to go back sixty years when I could say to someone who asked me what my profession is that I am a journalist and not be glared at. For even if the "media" of today are not admired as the "press" of yesterday, it is still a great and wonderful thing to work at finding out what the establishment does not want to tell you and to tell people who need to know.

What Are the Limitations on Freedom of the Press?†

I don't know why there is something more imposing about this speaking engagement than previous speaking engagements on this campus. I have spoken frequently in the School of Journalism and once in the School of Business, but somehow there is something about the law that intimidates me. Maybe that's because I've had a couple of brushes with the law. It is somehow different tonight. First of all, we're live on radio and we're being taped for campus television. That, of course, is intimidating itself.

Secondly, there is something about law school that makes it different than speaking on any other campus, and I guess it has to do with the word "law." It was two weeks ago that I got a letter from the Department of Justice telling me that after fifteen months I was no longer under investigation to see whether there was any kind of law to be thrown at me. It took a very long time before they decided there wasn't any. That, plus the fact that there was a point at which jail loomed as a rather imminent danger, makes me feel differently about the law.

I looked at the topic for tonight, "Limits on Freedom of the Press." Yesterday, I asked Dean Bailey of the Journalism School, "who the hell ever chose that as the topic?," and he looked at me and said, "You did." I don't know why I chose that topic, except possibly that it was bait for the law school people; I knew that it would appeal to them. The other possibility was that, having done a great deal of public speaking in the past several months, I was looking for a rest, and wanted to get up and say, "My subject tonight is the limits on freedom of the press. I don't think there should be any. Thank you very much."

Actually, when I did choose that subject it was because I had wanted to put out a deliberately provocative subject: "Why is a reporter talking about limits on freedom of press?" The answer is because he's the only safe person to talk about it. As soon as you get

---

† . This speech was originally published under the same title in the *Hastings Communications and Entertainment Law Journal* at 1 COMM/ENT L.J 175 (1977), *reprinted in* 18 HASTINGS COMM/ENT L.J. 441 (1996).

judges talking about it or congressmen talking about it, they talk about it in a somewhat more alarming context. My purpose tonight is to try to negotiate some kind of reasonable compromise with the law, to try to explain to you my view of what the permissible limits of freedom of press are. I don't expect that I'll have full concurrence with my views by everybody, but I rarely have full concurrence with my views anyway.

Let me say first that there have been threats to freedom of the press and that they don't come in the form of, "Let's threaten the freedom of press." They're almost always stated in terms of public values, usually quite legitimate values. The one I was confronted with came from Congress and had to do with the fact that the House of Representatives had decided that a report which had been drawn up by its own Select Committee on Intelligence, a report that this Committee had voted 9 to 4 to publish, should not be published. No member of the House outside the Committee itself had read the report, so the decision was not based on anything quite as rational as having gone into the subject and substance of it. It was a political decision. By political decision, I don't necessarily mean to be pejorative. The House of Representatives is a political body. It is politically elected and has political responsibilities.

They perceived, I think inaccurately, that they were in trouble because the investigations of the intelligence community had gone so far that a certain backlash had begun to build up. The White House began to make an election issue of this security-conscious Administration against a leaky House of Representatives, and there was a kind of panic in the House. In response to what they considered to be the mandate of their constituents, at least as represented by the American Legionnaires, they decided to forbid their own committee, to publish the report. Then, when I appeared to act in defiance of them and proceeded to publish a report that they did not publish, it became rather natural for them to pick me as a target amid a great deal of debate featuring the name of Benedict Arnold. Congressman Stratton of the State of New York, who introduced the resolution for a House investigation, told me himself that the initial idea was simply to have me cited for contempt of the House for having done what the House did not want done. And, weirdly enough, there exists a Supreme Court precedent allowing a chamber of Congress, if it feels that its legislative duties have been interfered with, to cite a citizen for contempt for obstructing its legislative process.[1] They sentence you to jail just like that. However, they discovered that because of Due Process it could only be done after a trial.[2]

They contemplated having a trial for me in the well of the House of Representatives and they went so far as to research that possibility. They then decided that was not exactly the way they wanted to go. They dropped the idea of a summary citation for contempt and decided instead first to investigate the source of the leak. They asked the House Judiciary Committee to do that and the Judiciary Committee said they would rather not. They then asked the House Rules Committee and they weren't really interested. So they found the House Ethics Committee, which later became very busy with Wayne Hays and other important matters. Up until that point the Ethics Committee had done nothing. And, I must say, first they tried to exercise their responsibility without crossing that tenuous line that separates the responsibility of Congress from the responsibility of the press.

They interviewed some four hundred witnesses including members and staff of the House, the staff of the Committee, and people from the CIA and elsewhere in the Executive Branch to see if they could trace the source of the leak without having to cross that constitutional Great Divide and call in a reporter to ask him, under the threat of contempt and jail, "Where did you get that report?" But they didn't succeed in the seven months of their investigation, and finally, they did call me.

The House Ethics Committee had been told to find out why it is that the House of Representatives can't keep its secrets. The only way they could find out was to go to somebody who had published the secret. That was their mission, that was their mandate, they regarded that as a legislative necessity and within the proper domain of the House of Representatives. The House couldn't perform its business, it couldn't keep its secrets, and if it required calling a reporter to find out why, that was what they were prepared to do. But perhaps without realizing it, they were invading constitutional rights.

So they called me and in the end we faced the moment where I was asked, "Where did you get that report?" They knew what was going to happen. I said, "I can't tell you." I was asked nine different

---

1. *See* Walkins v. United States, 354 U.S. 178, 215 (1957); Jurnoy v. MacCracken, 294 U.S. 125, 128 (1935).

2. *See Walkins*, 354 U.S. at 209.

ways, and nine different times. I was warned that my refusal to answer would subject me to a citation for contempt. It was a very serious matter and it had what we call a "chilling effect." Calling a reporter and subjecting him to the threat of contempt has to have a chilling effect on the exercise of our press freedoms. Had they succeeded and I'd gone to jail, it would have been a lot more chilling, especially for me.

We held them off. They didn't proceed, finally; they didn't have the votes on the floor of the House because public opinion had swung in the meanwhile. But it isn't as though you win a victory that stays won. It was one of the examples where Congress, perhaps not quite realizing what they'd done, had encroached on one of the really fundamental and sacred freedoms—freedom of the press—by trying to find out my source.

One of the other things I found out, traveling around our country, talking about this matter (and even occasionally listening), is that people who want to be supportive don't understand why some of these things which seem so small and parochial become so important. With a great many people I've talked to in various audiences the question arises, "If you think the public has a right to know everything, then why don't they have a right to know where you get your news?" That makes sense on the surface of it. They're very interested to know where you get something like that. They say, "Congress wants to know and they should know, and we want to know and, by the way, who was Deep Throat? Why can't we know things like this?"

There is a tension between various elements in our society. There is a natural wish of Congress and a natural curiosity of the people at large to understand everything they can. You have to understand that, however contradictory this sounds, there are certain things that those engaged in trying to give you all the information still have to keep secret.

It may seem to be a contradiction, but it really isn't because if you can't keep your source of information secret, you would not acquire the most essential information that you want to give. If on one occasion you are forced to betray a source that you promised to protect, then all your sources dry up. The entire system of unofficial communication of information begins to break down, and I think that system of unofficial communication is more important than people realize. You live today in an age with a great number of people not understanding other people, of groups in society which are set at sword's points, and part of the reason they are set at sword's points is that there are walls between people.

An example of this is the *Branzburg-Caldwell* case.[3] It involved a reporter named Earl Caldwell who was in touch with the Black Panthers. He wanted America to understand them. They obviously weren't going to go to the prosecutors, the police, or the FBI and talk about things which they had done that were illegal. They had a grievance, and if there was any way of ever bringing America together, it was for the large majority of the American people to understand a little bit about what drives more minorities to do such desperate things as carrying guns, making threats, and other illegal acts. Caldwell was a safety valve.

Another one of our safety valves, for Catholics, is to go to a priest and confess. Because a safety valve is so important, the law protects the right of the priest to keep confidential what he hears from the person who has confessed, even though it may involve something the police would like to know. In fact, the law itself, has the most sweeping protection of privilege, because, by God, lawyers wrote it. There's also a certain recognition of privilege with regard to doctors and their patients. The reason that this privilege exists is that if it didn't exist the whole system wouldn't work.

Now the fact of the matter is that certain alienated parts of America want to communicate to the rest of America because they need a long-range way to find some solutions to the problems that divide them. This rests on the ability to communicate in unofficial ways, and one of these is to say something to a reporter. They trust you, they tell you what's going on, and you don't tell the cops. Remember, if Caldwell knew he had to tell the cops then he would say to the Black Panthers, "Don't tell me because I'm going to be forced to tell."

If we're going to have a system in which reporters have to reveal their sources, then ideally they wouldn't have those sources. But then it is America which suffers. You could cut off that unofficial channel which crosses the barricades that exist between some groups in America and the majority of Americans. You just won't know what's going on. The first thing you'll know is that guns start going off or something else starts happening because there's been no communication. What is very hard for people connected with the law

---

3.   Branzburg v. Hayes, 408 U.S. 665 (1972).

to understand is the positive value of the kind of channel that exists through the press in this country.

That brings me to my main point. I am not an absolutist about these questions of press rights. I understand that there are various important values in this country. I understand the right of a free press versus the right to a fair trial. Some people say it's the First Amendment versus the Sixth Amendment, which guarantees the right to a fair trial. And we constantly run into trouble.

My problem was with Congress. For others it is the Executive Branch. When the Pentagon Papers reached the *New York Times*, the Justice Department, on behalf of President Nixon, went to the courts and tried to get an injunction against publication. If there's anything that should be important to this country, it is that there should be no prior restraint on publication. This went to the Supreme Court and there was a decision that wasn't all that wonderful, but it did permit the publication of the Pentagon Papers to go ahead.[4] However, if you read the decision carefully, the Court reached consensus only on the idea that there was nothing grave enough in the Pentagon Papers to warrant an injunction.[5] That, for a lot of people, is not a very happy solution to the problem because what it didn't give is an absolute statement that there can be no prior restraint. In fact, there was a suggestion that there could, under certain circumstances, be legally-valid prior restraint, that is, censorship in advance, telling you that you cannot publish something.[6]

Our main problem, oddly enough, is not with Congress, not with the Executive, but with the courts. That's strange since the courts, on the whole, have done a wonderful job of trying to protect American constitutional rights. Why is it then that we, who are trying to exercise those rights, argue with the courts? Why the gag orders in Nebraska[7] or the jailing of people in Fresno[8] because they refuse to reveal their sources? Why is it that the courts which, on the whole, have done a pretty good job of trying to maintain the rights of Americans, are up against the press, which is also trying in its own way to keep America free?

---

4. New York Times, Co. v. United States, 403 U.S. 713 (1971) (per curiam).
5. *Id.* at 719, 730.
6. *Id.* at 729, 733.
7. *See* Nebraska Press Ass'n v. Stuart, 427 U.S. 539 (1976).
8. *See* Rosato v. Superior Court, 124 Cal. Rptr. 427 (Cal. Ct. App. 5 Dist., 1975).

It is because the press, which can fight pretty well against a lot of other adversaries, finds it hard to fight the courts when they say that there is an argument between your Amendment and our Amendment, the First and the Sixth.[9] There's a tension between the need for justice and the need for public information.[10] And so we (meaning the courts) will decide that. This means that the courts, which are in a sense a party to a very important dispute, are also the referee in that dispute. They see things their way. The average judge tends to see the importance of being able to conduct his trial properly and he sometimes sees it as necessary to declare somebody in contempt or issue a gag order simply because he's trying to do his job. He understands something about our job, but he clearly, for quite human reasons, sees his job in more specific and clear terms. So when a judge says to you, "Look, I'm just trying to make sure everybody gets a fair trial," it would seem to be an unarguably just premise.

But, I submit, the premise is arguable. I would even go so far as to say that not in all cases is the conclusion of a fair trial the most important thing that could happen in this country. It sounds like a strange thing to say, but for many reasons a lot of trials don't end. If the evidence is tainted or if something happened and the judge feels the trial should not continue, then cases get thrown out and a lot of people who would be considered guilty in a general and moral sense, go free. So it isn't true that every person must get a complete trial. It isn't true that this is the only important value in American society.

Immunity was given to John Dean[11] and the special prosecutor, Archibald Cox, didn't like that because he thought it would interfere with his investigation.[12] He went before Judge Sirica and tried to get the public hearings of the Senate Watergate Committee stopped altogether.[13] Then he tried to get them held off television.[14] Finally, he

---

9. U.S. CONST. amend. I ("Congress shall make no law . . . abridging the freedom of speech, or of the press."); U.S. CONST. amend. VI ("In all criminal prosecutions, the accused shall enjoy the right to a speedy and public trial, by an impartial jury.").

10. *See* Robert Berger, *The "No-Source" Presumption: The Harshest Remedy*, 36 AM. L. REV. 603 (1987) (providing an evaluation between the need for justice and the need for public information). *See also* James C. Goodall, *Protecting Sources and Defending Libel Actions*, Series PLI Order No. 64-3792, June 19, 1986; *Branzburg*, 418 U.S. 364.

11. Application of U.S. Senate Select Committee on Presidential Campaign Activities, 361 F. Supp. 1270, 1272, 1282 (D.D.C. 1973).

12. *Cf. id.* at 1272, 1277. *See also* PATRICIA ANN O'CONNER, THE IRAN-CONTRA PUZZLE 60 (1987).

13. *Application of U.S. Senate Select Committee*, 361 F. Supp. at 1279.

14. *Id.*

went in with the suggestion that anybody who was given immunity, or partial immunity as Dean was, should at least have to testify behind closed doors[15] so that his testimony would not confuse the prosecution.[16] Sirica called a hearing and obviously had a very strong predilection towards granting that request, because judges believe in what other judges do. That's a normal thing. But the Senate Watergate Committee argued, "First of all, we think it's exceeding your powers to issue orders to Congress as to how it conducts its investigation."[17]

The argument was also made that it may well be more fundamentally important for America to find out what happened in Watergate than for one, two, three, four, or five people to go to jail. If the price of public information on something like that should happen to be that a couple of culprits go free, maybe that price is worth paying.

Today, in what is called a media age, there is nothing quite as important as how people perceive what is going on. And, while I don't think that in most cases the information prejudices trials, lawyers have a tendency to exaggerate. Lawyers always come in and say that if there is anything in the papers, their client can't get a fair trial. In most cases lawyers tend to exaggerate that and they'll admit it when you have a drink with them. But they have to make the argument.

There are very few examples where publicity has a demonstrable effect. In the case of the trial of John Mitchell and Maurice Stans before the Watergate trial and the investigation of Robert Vesco, it was claimed they couldn't possibly get a fair trial because of all the publicity it had been given. And, perhaps proving them right, they were acquitted.[18]

But there are a lot of things you can do. You can sequester a jury; you can change from one city to another.[19] There are a lot of things you can do before you have to resort to silencing the press. Now, I don't think that we should say without discussion that if a trial is involved the press has to take a back seat. Not always. I value fair trials; I value justice. But, I would submit that there is a very real value in American society right alongside the value of seeing justice done. They come into sharp conflict. There is a decision to make, and that

---

15. *Id.*

16. *Cf. id.* at 1278.

17. *Id.* at 1280, 1282.

18. United States v. Mitchell, 485 F.2d 1290 (2d Cir. 1973).

19. Rideau v. Louisiana, 373 U.S. 723, 726 (1963) (holding it is a denial of Due Process to refuse a request for change of venue because of TV publicity surrounding the trial).

decision need not always be that a fair trial is more important than free information simply because the one who decides is the judge.

Then, if so far I've talked about what I do not consider to be permissible limitations on freedom of the press, I owe it to you to say where I do see limitation on press freedoms as a necessary thing. I speak to many large groups and inevitably there arises the question, "Since you published the report and know a lot of things the CIA does wrong, is there no limit on disclosing the nation's secrets? Would you publish anything, would you broadcast anything you have?" This question involved a series of basic misunderstandings.

Behind that question, first of all, is an attribution of omniscience to me which isn't entirely warranted. It's not as if I can learn anything I want to know and then I decide what to broadcast and not to broadcast. As a matter of fact, most of the nation's secrets—and this may come as a big shock to you—I do not get to know. Those secrets which a reporter gets to know usually shouldn't have been secrets in the first place. The only reason you get to know this is that there is somebody in the government who says, "This is for the birds. It's an embarrassment; it's not a secret." Most of the secrets that come out are things that shouldn't have been a secret anyway.

When something reaches me as a reporter (I've said this before, and I don't know if it would be better understood in law school than it was in business school or a lot of other schools) the question has to be, "Would you publish anything you get? Would you reveal any of the nation's secrets, no matter what?" The first principle which I have to establish—and which is so very hard to establish—is that information that reaches me isn't a secret anymore by virtue of the fact that it has reached me. I am a reporter and don't represent the intelligence community or the Pentagon. I represent the public. When information reaches me it is already unsecret by virtue of the fact that I have it. Not only because of that; but because if I have it, I'm pretty sure Seymour Hersh has had it yesterday and the KGB last week. And not only because nothing reaches me which isn't probably available to other reporters, but also because it isn't my function or prerogative to classify information.

That has been so hard for me to get across to people. I am not a government official. I don't classify. My job is to find out what is going on the best I can. It is ipso facto (I got that phrase from law school) not a secret at the point when it reaches me.

Now everybody has questions about disclosure versus national security. I would submit to you that we have a very big government taking care of national security. And very strong courts are taking care of justice and gag orders. I think the real limitation that we have to consider on freedom of the press should be the exercise of responsibility by the press in matters where there isn't a big institution to provide protection.

What I'm talking about is the privacy of the average, individual citizen. I think that is being eroded a lot faster today than is national security. I think we live in an age of enormous public interest in gossip; and gossip implies prying into people's lives. And the press has become extremely adept at prying. They know what levers to push, the place to go to find out people's credit ratings; they know the people to call to find out who's sleeping with whom and what's going on. The result of this is that there is a great deal of material in some papers and some local stations that can only be classified as gossip damaging to individuals without any essential importance in terms of public information. I think of horrendous questions that arise in newspaper offices like, "Do we publish the name of a rape victim?" These are questions with which the Supreme Court is loath to interfere. They don't want to make freedom of the press issues out of them. But precisely because the legal protection of privacy is not very strong, I would say it's an area where the press must exercise its own responsibility, because there is nobody else to protect the average citizen except us.

I'll give you a couple of examples of problems that I face in that connection very early in my career as a Watergate investigator. I got a piece of information that was interesting it its own way. You recall that they had two bugs in the Watergate building in the Democratic headquarters, one on Larry O'Brien's phone which didn't work very well and another on the telephone in the office of Spencer Oliver, who was the Democratic liaison to state Democratic Committees.[20] He didn't spend a lot of time in the office and for some reason it was to his [Oliver's] phone that the girls went if they wanted to make private calls.[21] Oliver's secretary and various other secretaries around the office used to go in and use that phone.[22] Across the street in the

---

20. *See* Anthony Marro, *Deep Throat, Phone Home*, WASH. POST, Nov. 25, 1984 (Book World), at 5.
21. *Id.*
22. *Id.*

Howard Johnson Motel sat Alfred Baldwin III, a former FBI agent, and with earphones on his head and a typewriter, typing it all down.[23] He finished and made a report, which was called the Gemstone Report, and brought a copy over to the Committee to Reelect the President.[24] A copy went over to H.R. Haldeman at the White House, and eventually a copy ended up in the office of the prosecutor when they began investigating; and since I had friends, I got to see a copy of it.

Gemstone had nothing in it of any political importance. There was nothing in it that had to do with the campaign or anything like that. But there was an awful lot of girls talking to friends about how they scored last night. And I looked at this material and said, "Is this news?"

If you want to know for what they spent a quarter of a million dollars, got seven people arrested, and the Nixon Administration overthrown, it was for a couple of secretaries talking about how they got laid. In a sense it had a kind of marginal interest. But I decided there was an interest in protecting the people whose privacy was being violated by being wiretapped and that for me to make a story about it would represent a further invasion of their privacy. And while it would be a great story for the *National Enquirer*, I decided to forget the story.

Occasionally there are borderline stories to worry about. I had a terrible problem when I came across the fact that the Senate Intelligence Committee was investigating assassinations. One of the biggest questions was what the presidents knew about assassination. You don't find in the files of the White House a memo in which President Kennedy says, "I want Castro bumped off. Please report before the close of business on Friday." They don't write those kinds of memos. The Senate Intelligence Committee had a great deal of trouble trying to find out to what extent the CIA was acting on its own and to what extent it responded to Presidential orders. That meant a peculiar problem at one point.

The CIA had been involved with the Mafia in trying to assassinate Fidel Castro.[25] There was a Mafia girl by the name of Judy Campbell. She met President Kennedy and he used to go to bed with her all the time at the Mayflower Hotel in Washington. The Committee was

---

23. *Id.*
24. *Id.*
25. *See Hall of Shame; Stuff and Nonsense,* INSIGHT MAG., Mar. 19, 1992, at 27.

looking into that only because of the questions, "Could Kennedy have known from her, since she was a friend of the Mafia? Could they have discussed the assassination of Castro, in which case Kennedy would have known." They finally decided that they probably had not. That is to say, they had testimony that she didn't know about the assassination plots, whatever other subject they might have discussed.

But I had the problem that, on a tip from the Senate Intelligence Committee, I got to know about President Kennedy and Judy Campbell. And I hate stories about Presidents and their private lives. I just hate that kind of story. Suppose it was a story about the President being blackmailed by the mafia or a story about whether the President knew about assassinations. That would be a different story. I agonized about it because sometimes the distinction between an invasion of privacy and a *necessary* invasion of privacy is important if the country is to know what is going on in government. This isn't an easy question. But what I'm trying to say is that these are day-to-day decisions; they come up in various forms and aren't always easy.

I wish we had a better understanding with the courts and the legal profession. I would like to try to understand their problems and I wish they had a better understanding of the needs of those who provide public information. And I think that might happen, I think there might be something afoot. There are a whole lot of stories which newspaper people voluntarily agree to forget. There are a lot of appeals that can be made to the press without the threat of jail and gag orders. For example, we could hold off a day on a story, or not give part of it too much attention, because it would scare away a witness.

I think that in our society, whenever you're trying to find an absolute solution, something goes wrong. You violate somebody's rights and somebody ends up a revolutionary. In most cases, there are accommodations that could be reached once you get sufficient understanding. I want you lawyers to know that I'm willing to understand your needs; but don't arbitrarily impose your needs on us just because you have control over the writing of the laws and control of the courts. Don't arbitrarily impose your needs on us and send some reporters to jail—this will accomplish nothing. They'll go to jail, most of them, and stay there because they have to stay there. In this country, the rule of law will not survive unless the press is free enough so that this country knows what is going on.

The FBI and Me[†]

The FBI file on the famous "investigation" has now been released.

On June 4, 1973, President Nixon sat in the Oval Office, earphones on his head, listening to tapes, making running observations to Alexander Haig and Ron Ziegler. He listened to himself suggesting three months earlier, on March 13, to John Dean, then still his agent, that it should be maintained that he had used the FBI "only for national security purposes."[1]

As he listened, Mr. Nixon commented. "Yeah. The only exception, of course, was that son-of-a-bitch Schorr. But there—actually it was national security. (Laughs) We didn't say that. Oh, we didn't do anything. We just ran a name check on the son-of-a-bitch."

Maybe a name check was what the former President wanted. What he got was a full field investigation, frantically aborted, then covered up with a bogus explanation. What he also got was one more item in the impeachment litany.

It was Item 65 in the Statement of Information on Surveillance Activities. It was Paragraph E in the Summary of Information on Illegal Intelligence Gathering. Finally, in the Judiciary Committee's Report to the House of Representatives,[2] it was one of the instances of abuse of presidential powers listed in Article II.[3]

I have recently been able to supplement the Judiciary Committee's extensive research and testimony with material from the files of the FBI, and finally have been able to piece together a comprehensive account of my mini-Watergate experience as seen from within the Nixon Administration.

That account I now offer because there are lessons about government-press relations that should not be lost in the general movement toward Watergate amnesia. The "son-of-a-bitch" reflex of a

---

[†]. This article was originally published under the same title at COLUM. JOURN. REV. 8 (Nov./Dec. 1974). Reprinted with permission.

1. SUBMISSION OF RECORDED PRESIDENTIAL CONVERSATIONS TO THE COMMITTEE ON THE JUDICIARY OF THE HOUSE OF REPRESENTATIVES BY PRESIDENT RICHARD NIXON 111-156 (Apr. 30, 1974).

2. H.R. REP. NO. 93-1305 (1974).

3. *See id.* at 150-51 (section of the Articles of Impeachment entitled "Daniel Schorr FBI Investigation").

president toward an offending newsman did not start, and probably will not end with Nixon. But, for once, it is possible to document how presidential powers were abused in intended retaliation in ways that could occur again.

The Judiciary Committee's Report summed up the operation:

DANIEL SCHORR FBI INVESTIGATION

In August, 1971, Daniel Schorr, a television commentator for the Columbia Broadcasting System, was invited to the White House to meet with the President's staff assistants to discuss an unfavorable analysis he had made of a presidential speech. Shortly thereafter, Haldeman instructed his chief aide, Higby, to obtain an FBI background report on Schorr. The FBI conducted an extensive investigation of Schorr, interviewing twenty-five people in seven hours, including Schorr's friends and employers, and members of his family. When press reports revealed that the investigation had taken place, the President's aides fabricated and released to the press the explanation that Schorr was being considered for an appointment as an assistant to the chairman of the Council on Environmental Quality. The President knew that Schorr had never been considered for any government position. The President approved the cover story. Haldeman has testified that although he could not remember why the investigation was requested, Schorr was not being considered for federal employment.[4]

The FBI investigation—like my appearance on White House "enemy" lists—did me no ultimate harm, thanks, perhaps, to the ineptitude with which it was handled. But in the period after I became aware of it, the episode had its disconcerting if not "chilling" effects. It complicated my relations with my employer and my news sources. I had to worry about being projected into an undesired role of administration adversary.

That concern persists. For that reason, I have waived any suit on invasion of privacy or other grounds, uncomfortable with the idea of a docket headed, *Daniel Schorr v. Richard M. Nixon.* But I did want information, and I concluded, in consultation with J. Roger Wollenberg of the Washington law firm of Wilmer, Cutler & Pickering, that the Freedom of Information Act[5] provided the appropriate vehicle.

On March 19, we applied to Clarence M. Kelley, Director of the FBI, for all material in the FBI's file dealing with the investigation of me, specifically excluding interviews and summaries since I had no desire to violate the privacy of those contacted about me.

---

4. *Id.*

5. 5 U.S.C. § 552 (1994).

On March 27, Kelley rejected the request on the ground that "investigations concerning possible presidential appointments are considered to be investigatory material compiled for law enforcement purposes and thereby exempt from disclosure." One could only marvel that, at this late date, Kelley could still be talking about "possible presidential appointments."

On April 24, we appealed to Attorney General William Saxbe, pointing out that this investigation was not conducted for legitimate law enforcement purposes, and therefore could not be exempt from disclosure.

On June 6, Saxbe, overruling the FBI director, advised that the file would be released to me "as a matter of administrative discretion." It was delivered to Wollenberg on July 2.

The FBI investigation was set in motion on August 19, 1971, two days after I had broadcast on the *CBS Evening News* an analysis suggesting that President Nixon's promise to come to the rescue of the financially beleaguered Catholic parochial schools represented political rhetoric, unsupported by any concrete program.

The House Judiciary Committee quotes Haldeman assistant Lawrence Higby as testifying that, traveling with President Nixon and H. R. Haldeman on August 19 over Wyoming, on a cross-country trip to California, he called FBI Director J. Edgar Hoover, as instructed by Haldeman, to ask for "a complete background" on me, and was later surprised to learn that the FBI had launched a full-field investigation of "the poor guy."

Higby may have been taken aback by the wide-open nature of the investigation, but could hardly have been surprised by the fact that it had taken place. For, promptly after receiving his request, Hoover wrote him on August 20, "I am enclosing a memorandum of what our files show on Daniel Louis Schorr. I have also initiated a complete investigation of Schorr and, as soon as it is completed, I will forward it to you."

However Higby couched his request to the late director, Hoover from the outset treated it as a crash investigation preceding a presidential appointment. His first instruction, on August 19, headed, "Daniel Louis Schorr, Special Inquiry," required a completed report by August 23 "without fail," and said, "The President has requested extremely expedite applicant-type investigation of Schorr, who is being considered for presidential appointment, position not stated. Do not indicate White House interest to persons contacted."

That message went to the FBI representative in the American Embassy in Bonn. It referred to a Who's Who biography that listed me as Chief, CBS News bureau for Germany and Central Europe, which I had indeed been until 1966. I might have been more conscientious about keeping Who's Who up to date had I dreamed that the FBI might not be aware I had been working in Washington for five years, my presence no secret to other government agencies and to TV audiences.

Next, the FBI sent telegrams to its field offices in Washington, New York, St. Louis, Baltimore and Alexandria, Virginia, asking "identities and locations of all close relatives. . . . Make certain all periods of adult life are accounted for." The telegrams included new information, "Note: Schorr is now in U.S."

It took until the next morning before the FBI learned that I was not just visiting. An August 20 memorandum said, "Investigation this morning indicates Schorr has been transferred back to the United States and is presently residing in Washington, D.C., with his family. He is apparently assigned to the CBS Washington bureau."

The picture of the FBI, like the Keystone Cops, charging off first in the wrong direction to Germany has its humorous side. But it also suggests that the White House did not tell Hoover the real motive for the investigation.

Interviews about my background were going forward in the United States and abroad, but in Washington, where I had finally been located, the FBI ran into trouble. The Washington field office advised that William Small, then Washington bureau chief of CBS News, when contacted about the "job" investigation, stated that "he was shocked to hear this as he had no indication that Schorr was being considered for any federal position."

Well, I might not necessarily have told CBS of my plans to join President Nixon's team. But other FBI reports quoted me as saying I knew of no prospective position. Puzzled, the FBI got in touch with Higby, now in San Clemente with Mr. Nixon. One can picture the astonishment. An FBI memo said, "Higby . . . advised that in view of these developments, the FBI should discontinue its investigation until we hear further from Higby."

To FBI field offices went crisp, telegrams, "Discontinue investigation immediately."

But in the seven hours that the investigation had been "active," twenty-five interviews had been conducted, and the information already collected was ordered transmitted to headquarters. After a weekend of reflection, Higby called on Monday, August 23, saying, according to an FBI memo, "The investigation should be canceled; however, requested that all information developed by the bureau to date concerning Schorr be furnished his [Higby's] office."

The same day Hoover wrote Higby enclosing "a summary memorandum containing the results of the investigation." And, doggedly sticking to its bureaucratic guns, the bureau furnished for Hoover's file "one copy of a biographical resume concerning the appointee." I have asked that the file be expunged. Director Kelley says that, under regulations, he can't.

There the matter rested, the White House and FBI presumably hoping the case was closed.

On November 10, storm, signals went up. Assistant Director T. E. Bishop, in charge of public relations, reported in a memorandum to his superiors that he had been called by "Ken Clawson, a reporter for the *Washington Post*, who, is well known to the bureau," asking about the August investigation.

"Clawson advised Bishop," wrote Bishop,

> that the FBI might not realize it, but the FBI had been 'used' by someone in the White House in connection with its investigation of Schorr. . . . Clawson said that he has been informed by a source in the White House that Schorr was never being considered for appointment to a government position and that the individual who had made the request of the FBI was aware of this but had asked the FBI to conduct an investigation, allegedly in connection with possible employment, but actually for the purpose of getting background information on Schorr in an expedite manner.

If there was concern about possible misuse of the FBI, it is nowhere evident in the FBI file. The alarm was about impending adverse publicity. The next step was to coordinate with the White House. Here is Hoover's memorandum of a telephone conversation at 4:18 p.m. on November 10:

> Honorable H. R. Haldeman, Assistant to the President, called. He said that as I may know, the *Washington Post* is cranking up a story on an FBI investigation of CBS correspondent Daniel Schorr and apparently the bureau has confirmed to Ken Clawson, a reporter for the *Washington Post*, that such an investigation was ordered by the White House.
>
> I commented I would doubt that because my orders are to not give Clawson the time of day. Mr. Haldeman said he would be surprised if we had, but Clawson claims that he does have this confirmation from the Bureau and in any event he is going

apparently with the story that the White House is investigating this reporter.

Mr. Haldeman said that I may recall that there was a request for a check on him back in the middle of August and obviously the White House would have no useful purpose in getting any more publicity on it than necessary so that what he wanted to do was to be sure that we did not supply Clawson or any of the rest of the press with anything.

I told Mr. Haldeman my standing orders are not to give the time of day to him and I will check on it right away. Mr. Haldeman said that Ron Ziegler, Press Secretary, is concerned that they are going to create a repression of newsmen type of thing. I said that is the usual line.

Mr. Haldeman said he thought they would slough it off over there and if they ask any question, say they would not have anything to say as obviously information is sought on individuals at various times for various reasons such as appointments, routine checks, et cetera, and not have anything more to say and he assumes that is the position the Bureau would take.

I said we will not have anything to say and I would check and let him know as it may have been confirmed by the Public Information Office of the Department of Justice.

Clawson's story appeared on the front page of the *Washington Post* on November 11, and was widely quoted by news agencies. The White House moved to develop its cover story. President Nixon met with his special counsel, Charles Colson.

Before the House Judiciary Committee, Colson testified that "the suggestion was made that we respond to press inquiries by stating that he [Schorr] was being considered for a position as a press or a television consultant on matters of environmental . . . environmental matters." Committee Counsel John Doar interrogated Colson:

Doar: The fact was that Mr. Schorr was not nor hadn't been considered for such a position?

Colson: That is right.

Doar: And the President knew this?

Colson: Yes, sir.

Doar: And you knew this?

Colson: I did.

Doar: And Mr. Haldeman knew this?

Colson: That is correct.

Doar: And that you were directed by the President to implement the instructions by putting out this information that Mr. Schorr was being considered for a job.

Colson: I don't know that I was instructed to put out the information, but it was decided that that would be the response and I think Mr. Ziegler actually gave that response.

Doar: When you say it was decided, you are speaking, that is a colloquialism to mean that the President decided. Isn't that fair?

Colson: Well, it is not a general colloquialism. In this case it is.

Doar: That the President decided it?

Colson: I think the President and I decided that that would be the best way that we could work ourselves out of what looked like an embarrassing situation. . . . We decided that this would be an appropriate way to dig ourselves out of a political hole. It may very well be that I said we ought to put this out, and the President said, 'fine.' It may be that he said to me, why don't you talk to Ziegler and see if we can give this as an answer.

The next day, November 12, was a busy day at the FBI. Senator Sam Ervin was proposing a hearing of his Constitutional Rights Subcommittee, and Chairman Emanuel Celler of the House Judiciary Committee wrote Attorney General John Mitchell, asking for an explanation. While preparing to join the White House in the cover-up, the bureau was busy protecting its own flank.

Hoover sent a memorandum to Mitchell summarizing the situation and displaying his own clean hands. Hoover wrote:

When we were originally requested to investigate Daniel Schorr last August by Mr. Higby, an assistant to Mr. Haldeman, it was indicated to us that he was being considered for an important position. There was no mention at any time relative to the White House being curious about the background of Schorr because of some unfavorable articles; which he had written about the President and members of the White House staff.

Presidential Counsel John Dean visited the FBI with a lot of questions about investigation procedures to help prepare a plausible position. As summarized in an FBI memo, Dean wanted to know whether there were precedents for investigations initiated before jobs were offered, whether the FBI ever disclosed the White House as the instigator of an investigation, whether the FBI would respond if questioned by a congressional committee. The replies were all reassuring, and W. R. Wannall, supervising special agent in the intelligence division, wrote that Dean did not "make or imply any criticism of the bureau's handling of this case." Nor, apparently, did the FBI express any criticism whatever of the White House's handling of the case, except internally.

Wrote Wannall:

It was, however, apparent from the discussion. that someone at the White House got their signals mixed and requested a full field investigation when, in fact, probably all they wanted was background information on Schorr and a check of FBI files similar to that which has previously been requested by Haldeman's office on other news personalities.

This was the first suggestion that I was not the first newsman Haldeman had asked the FBI to look into. Interestingly, this was the only point commented on when the FBI's legal counsel, John. A. Mintz, undertook personally to deliver the FBI file to my lawyer, Roger Wollenberg. Mintz, calling attention to the reference to "other news personalities," volunteered that this meant routine name checks of the type made for credential purposes or for screening White House visitors. But, when Wollenberg asked whether Mintz could represent officially that no other Haldeman instigated full investigations of newsmen had been made, Mintz said, "We do not know." Since then the FBI has stated, "We will not furnish, affirm or acknowledge the identities of individuals on whom name checks have been made."

With the information John Dean had brought back to the White House, the President's position was formulated. A news conference was called for late in the afternoon, and Mr. Nixon was ready to respond to an anticipated question. Hoover got a phone call from Haldeman with advance word of what the President would say, summarized as follows in Hoover's memo:

> . . . [the President] understands Mr. Schorr was being considered for a public affairs position in the area of environmental matters and there was a routine FBI investigation, but there was nothing detrimental; that the position was not offered; that no one can object to the FBI check being given him the same as to anyone else, and the only objection seems to be that he was not asked beforehand if he were interested, and that objection, to the President, makes sense: and accordingly he has ordered that whenever anyone is being considered for a Government position, he be informed beforehand and if he is not interested, consideration would be dropped; that there was no intimidation nor will there be, and to make sure, he has directed this additional safeguard be instituted.

"I told Mr. Haldeman that was a good statement," Hoover wrote. "Mr. Haldeman says it does put the burden that before any check is run on anybody, he has to be notified, but he did not think that harms them any. I agreed."

Hoover's memo concludes, "Mr. Haldeman thanked me."

As luck would have it, Mr. Nixon's November 12 news conference was dominated by questions about Vietnam, and no one asked about my investigation. So, afterward, Ziegler sought out reporters and told them what the President would have said had he been asked. The wire services moved that as a story separate from the news conference.

One version caused Ziegler to make a speedy call to Hoover. Ziegler, according to Hoover's memo, said he:

> understood that the UPI would carry a story to the effect that the President had said that the investigation of Daniel Schorr had been clumsily handled. Mr. Ziegler wanted to assure me that no such statement had been made by the President and the proposed story by the United Press would be inaccurate.

Clearly, this was no time to alienate Hoover.

Peace descended on the Schorr file in the FBI for a time. Then there was a new flurry of paper at the end of 1971. The Department of the Army, which had sounded me out about speaking at the 1972 annual War College seminar, asked the FBI for one of those routine "name checks." But nothing about me seemed routine to the FBI. It referred the Army to the White House, and on January 5, 1972, Hoover advised Haldeman in a letter, "[w]e are making no comment concerning the investigation we conducted regarding Mr. Schorr, and the Department of the Army is being referred to the White House." What the White House told the Army, I do not know, but the invitation to the War College never came.

Activity in the FBI stirred anew at the end of January as Senator Ervin prepared to hold a hearing on February 1. Confronted with an Ervin letter asking details about my investigation, the FBI, in a January 6 internal memo, recalled the promise to Presidential Counsel Dean not to cooperate with any congressional inquiry, but said that since "our relationship with the Senator has been very cordial in the past," it might be well to be "responsive to his inquiries."

Back came John Dean to the FBI to work things out. According to Agent Wannall's memo:

> Dean advised that Clark MacGregor, Counsel to the President for Congressional Relations, had gone to see Ervin and asked him in effect "what would call him off.". . . Ervin indicated to MacGregor that in the past, situations have arisen in which the FBI has presented the facts to him which have fully satisfied his interest in a particular matter. . . . Dean feels that a letter to Ervin simply stating the facts might well close this matter as far as Ervin is concerned. Dean said that in view of the extreme sensitivity of this matter to the White House, the White House would like to have the opportunity to review our letter to Ervin before it is sent.

Dean later advised that he had discussed the draft letter with Haldeman, who suggested no changes. Hoover also sent a copy to Attorney General Mitchell, noting that it had been "cleared with Honorable H.R. Haldeman and Honorable John M. Dean III of the White House."

So, in a January 27 letter, Hoover assured Senator Ervin that "the investigation was requested as a routine background investigation for possible federal appointment in which we make inquires regarding a person's character, loyalty, general standing, and ability. The incomplete investigation of Mr. Schorr was entirely favorable to him and the results were furnished to the White House."

Hoover, of course, knew a lot more, but was not about to rock the boat. Senator Ervin accepted his explanation at face value. The last document in the FBI file, as released to me, is a letter from Ervin to Hoover on February 3, saying, "[t]he FBI certainly did not do anything except its legal duty in initiating the investigation of Mr. Schorr at the insistence of some official in the White House."

So, my mini-Watergate conformed to the pattern of the larger Watergate conspiracy—the plot, the goof, the cover-up. The fourth element—the unraveling—was to come some sixteen months later in the testimony of Dean and Haldeman before the Senate Watergate Committee.

I know now that Mr. Nixon himself wanted an FBI report on me, for reasons that can only be surmised, and that he personally approved the cover-up plan suggested by Colson. What I have not known until now is how far the FBI went in cooperating with the cover-up, and how little concern it showed about the White House abuse of its investigative powers.

There remains to be investigated, though Mr. Nixon said I was "the only exception," what other newsmen Haldeman had the FBI investigate.

Why did the White House's desire for a quiet, covert investigation of me became translated by Hoover into A wide-open full-field job investigation that brought embarrassment to the White House? I still do not have the answer, and perhaps, with Hoover dead, I never shall.

My mini-Watergate was only one facet in a much larger picture. But I recall the remark of Max Frankel, then Washington bureau chief of the *New York Times*, who knew about the FBI investigation of me from the outset.

"I'll never forgive myself," he said, "for not sensing that such an investigation could not be an isolated event but had to be part of something much bigger."

But, if Mr. Nixon did not succeed in what he originally had in mind, he did accomplish one thing. He made me part of the story instead of simply the observer. He forced me to submit to a thousand jokes about whether my FBI "shadow" was still with me, and whether it was safe to talk to me on the telephone. He made me worry about whether I was still perceived by the public as an objective reporter, and whether I might be a source of embarrassment to my own news organization in its conflicts with the government.

There are many kinds of "chilling effects" on the exercise of press freedom. Whenever a president uses the powers entrusted to him to go after a reporter, there are bound to be some.

Manipulation and the Media†

Before I get into my main subject, a word on current events:

Some may wonder what I am doing talking way up here while an investigation in which I seem to be a key figure is in progress on Capitol Hill. The short answer is that talking here is nicer. The longer answer is that while, obviously curious and concerned about the hearings being held by the House Ethics Committee, which has been trying for months to discover how I obtained the suppressed report of the House Intelligence Committee, I have no intention of cooperating in that venture.

I am not willing, by my uncommanded presence, to associate myself with an investigation whose purpose I deplore and whose effect can only be chilling to a free press. I take some comfort from the latest unanimous decision of the United States Supreme Court striking down a judicial gag order in Nebraska.[1] A concurring opinion underlined "the cleansing effects of exposure and accountability."[2] And while the reference was to the press and the courts, it applies equally to the press and the Executive and to the press and Congress. As the late great Justice Hugo Black put it in his opinion in the 1971 Pentagon Papers case,[3] "The press was protected so that it could bare the secrets of government and inform the people."[4] Which, I might add, would not work if the government could mandate what secrets could be bared.

So, I have previously declined an informal request, transmitted through my counsel, Joseph Califano, to be interviewed by the Ethics Committee staff. In the current hearings, I shall not appear unless subpoenaed. If subpoenaed, I shall not give any testimony about the

---

†. This speech was first presented as the Fourth Annual Lecture by Daniel Schorr, Paepcke Auditorium, Aspen Institute for Humanistic Studies, Aspen, Colorado, July 22, 1976.

1. Nebraska Press Ass'n v. Stuart, 427 U.S. 539 (1976). In *Stuart,* the Supreme Court struck down a Nebraska state trial judge's order entered in anticipation of a trial for a multiple murder, which had attracted widespread news coverage. The order enjoined the news media from publishing or broadcasting accounts of confessions or admissions made by defendant to law enforcement officers or third parties, except members of the press, and other facts "strongly implicative" of the defendant. *Id.*

2. *Id.* at 586 (Brennan, J., concurring).

3. New York Times, Co. v. United States, 403 U.S. 713 (1971) (per curiam).

4. *Id.* at 717.

source of the House Intelligence Report, or the source of any other information.

I use categoric language not to appear defiant or uncooperative, but to avoid any possible misunderstanding on what, to me, is a vital principle. If one reporter—especially in such a widely publicized case—were to betray a source that the reporter had promised to protect, then many sources would dry up for many reporters. And many Watergates and other scandals would go undetected.

When confidential sources evaporate, the reporter and the news organization are the first losers. But the public is the greater loser. And the nation and its free institutions, which depend on the vigilant probing of official actions, are the ultimate and the greatest losers.

I hope there will be no confrontation with Congress over sources. I hope that I shall not be asked my source and, if asked, that I can persuade the Ethics Committee of the reasons for not being able to furnish it. I hope that the Committee will not invoke its power to seek a citation for contempt.

I mean no contempt. As the Ethics Committee seeks to enforce Congressional ethics, so I must observe a journalist's ethic. I cannot— and I mean this in an almost visceral sense—I cannot go back on the professional standards of a lifetime. I cannot betray a news source.

These preliminary remarks are not entirely a digression from tonight's subject. They point up the intense public focus on the media. In Washington's Gridiron dinner, where print journalists traditionally lampoon the high and mighty in government, this year they lampooned a journalist—namely me. There was a skit featuring Clark Mollenhoff singing, to a House Intelligence Committee chairman, a song that ran, "I want a leak just like the leak they gave to dear old Dan!"

There is a national preoccupation today with what the press does, how it does it—and to whom. Part of that preoccupation is with the print press. The Woodward-Bernstein techniques of investigation compete successfully, in public interest, with the FBI's techniques of investigation, including the illegal ones. Seymour Hersh, who has exposed everything from the My Lai massacre to a Los Angeles wheeler-dealer, has become an almost mystical figure (if you can conceive of a mystical figure who is generally in tennis shoes).

But there is a special American fascination with personalities recognized from the Tube. How the Pentagon budgets its money to launch the cruise missile is far overshadowed in general public interest by how ABC budgets its money to launch Barbara Walters. How long

President Ford will hold out, and who will succeed him, are questions of great public interest—and almost as great are the same questions applied to Walter Cronkite.

Not in the same league with the fabulous television anchor persons, the reporters in television also come in for unusual interest because they become distinct figures, and symbols, in the public mind. For example, I doubt that the controversy over my CIA reporting would have reached its amazing proportions were it not somehow connected with my role as a television "personality." Nor, probably, would I have merited inclusion in the "top twenty" of Nixon enemies, with the notation, "A real media enemy." Nor might I have merited a special White House-instigated FBI investigation, a mini-Watergate complete with mini-cover-up of a fictitious job offer. Nor, perhaps, would I have been treated to public epithets by the former director of the CIA. That all these things happened to me may have had something to do with my personality, but they also had to do with the fact that I was a television personality.

Americans today are fascinated by television, and they are most ambivalent about their fascination. They will, on the one hand, vote for Walter Cronkite as their ranking symbol of trust and confidence— over any politician—and, at the same time, express profound unease about the power of television journalism. When I caused to have published the report of the House Intelligence Committee which the House had voted *not* to publish in that form, the burden of criticism was that, as a television newsman, I had reached some new height of arrogance by flouting the will of America's elected representatives. Yet, in essence, I had only done what Neil Sheehan and the *New York Times* had done with the Pentagon Papers—determined that a document, once out of Government control, could not be recalled, be it by the Attorney General, in that case, or by the House of Representatives, in my case.[5] But, in my case, there was clearly an overlay of widespread feeling about the alleged power of television journalists to govern events and people's lives.

We have heard a great deal in recent years about the "power of the media," and not just from former Vice President Agnew who, as we now know, was seeking to exploit the widespread unease about broadcast news for the benefit of a Nixon conspiracy to discredit the television press. My thought today is that the unease about television and the fear of manipulation is too undifferentiated. It confuses the

---

5. *See id.*

impact of television as a means of communication, which is enormous, with the impact of television *journalism*, which is quite moderate.

There is no doubt that the pervasiveness of television has changed our consciousness. It has vastly accelerated the process of trend-setting and trend-changing. It has created, and it has destroyed, idols and images overnight. It has tended to emphasize concrete audio-visual images over abstract ideas. Sometimes, it seems to blur the line between the real and the unreal.

Let me give you one example from my Pike Report experience. Several times I displayed a copy of the Pike Report on television, referring to it as "the unreleased report," "the secret report" and, finally, "the suppressed report." Yet there was not a single telephone call or letter asking how come, if this report was secret, I was showing it on television? I inquired about that curious lack of reaction after the controversy exploded. People generally said they weren't sure I was really showing the report. Some said they are so confused by all the visual aids on television, that they are no longer certain what is actual and what is a piece of graphic art.

The confusion, I believe, goes much further. When fiction is presented with a documentary technique and news events become so incredible as to rival fiction, it takes an effort of concentration to distinguish between one and the other. I am sure that some who saw the Senate Watergate hearings instead of their soap operas came to regard the hearings as some other kind of soap opera. I am sure that when people sometimes are slow to react to accidents and muggings taking place before their eyes, it is because some are no longer sure it is something really happening and not another fleeting image on the television screen.

Recently, a woman wrote Columnist Ann Landers that she had been robbed by an armed bandit, who left her bound and gagged, telling her four-year-old son to turn on the television and not call for help until the program was over. That would be in twenty minutes allowing time for a getaway. For the next three hours the boy watched television, ignoring his mother's struggle to get his attention. I suspect that, to the boy, his mother's muffled screams were no more real than the television show.

I believe that television, not as a conspiracy but as a phenomenon, has altered our collective personality, making us generally more passive, waiting to receive images, yet distrustful of the images we receive. Television presents, on the same tube, without warnings on the package, such a bewildering medley of fact and fiction, and something in between, that, for many, the basic distinction between reality and unreality has been blurred.

Indeed, television, because of its power and pervasiveness, can create its own reality which, in pragmatic terms, may be more important than the old objective reality.

The journalists, occupying a small corner of this mansion, strain to present facts with tools better designed for fantasy. A constant battle is fought against the temptations to staging, re-enactment, false images, tendentious excerpting for dramatic effect. Fought, I say, and not always won. There are alterations of reality, under the tyranny of techniques, which become almost unconscious. Like the "listening shot," needed for editing, but usually filmed after the interview showing the listener not quite as he was when he was really listening. Like the editing of speeches, testimony and interviews, in the interests of time, to get the most telling point, but eliminating digressions, pauses, and uncertainty, and thus making all public figures terse and sharply-focused, which, if I am not revealing another secret, not all of them are. Sometimes I think that television news is like an allegory, using a conventional form to arrive, as briefly and dramatically as possible, at a basic truth. That so much truth survives is a credit to the news organizations coping with the medium.

But, with all the good intentions in the world, some things cannot be controlled. Vital issues—hunger, pollution—are dramatized on television to a saturation point, and often public attention burns out before there are solutions.

That is a result of the pervasiveness, not the perversity of television journalism. Because journalism on television requires sharply-defined viewpoints, there is a tendency to create polarization around extremes, sometimes overlooking the middle ground where the truth often lies.

Network television journalists, on the whole, are not seeking to manipulate the news, but to keep abreast of it and steer it through the electronic shoals. If they sometimes seem in sovereign control of the events they describe, that is largely another illusion created by television. I never realized, until I heard a scholarly study here in Aspen, that the convention of placing the correspondent against a background of the White House or Congress creates the subliminal effect, over a period of time, that the correspondent overshadows these institutions dwindling into the background. That is one of the things I mean when I differentiate between the *television* effect and the *journalistic* effect. Another example: A live event on television—a political convention, a shoot-out between police and the Symbionese Liberation Army—has enormous impact. But I doubt that the broadcaster who introduces and narrates the event has much additional impact. Indeed, when the narration differs from the viewer's perception, the switchboard may quickly light up. On television, the journalist, is, on the whole, much less vivid than the actuality, though, as the messenger, he may be credited or blamed—usually blamed—for the event.

On scheduled news broadcasts, journalistic decisions obviously play a greater role. The stories are selected, the time for each allotted, the film excerpts are chosen. Editors on television do what editors on newspapers have done for centuries without arousing comparable public emotion and charges of slanting. It isn't quite the same, of course. With fewer stories, a bigger audience and greater vividness, the television news decisions become more critical than the newspaper's. A TV story gets pushed not from Page One to Page Two, but from the front page into oblivion. Or, with luck, to the Morning News. So, when most Americans get most of their idea of the daily world from three nightly news broadcasts, it is understandable that they worry about the power that Cronkite and Chancellor-Brinkley and Reasoner-Walters seem to wield. In fact, anchor personalities are mainly institutional show windows for news-gathering, news-presenting organizations. But, the show window is an important thing in television, and apparently television wouldn't have it any other way. Because the anchor person sits there, confident, serene, omniscient, he/she appears to be in full charge and fully able to manipulate the public in any way he/she desires. That was the image that Agnew so successfully exploited as part of, as we later learned from Watergate, a conspiracy to discredit the press and thus facilitate other conspiracies.

But, let me suggest to you that the real problem is not manipulation *by* television, but manipulation *of* television by others. Television is more and more confronted with staged events, semi-events and pseudo-events designed for little more than to get on television. During the recent California primary fight, Roger Mudd did a telling little piece of analysis about Ronald Reagan and Jerry Brown, rushing around to appear before little groups so that these media events would get on television and reach millions more. It goes further. Legislative hearings in Congress are scheduled for maximum television exposure (except when minimum exposure is desired). I can recall the staff director of a Senate committee who offered to postpone a hearing, when I told him that, because of competing events, we would not be able to cover. I can recall Senator Humphrey, meeting me in the hall, and bemoaning the fact that a vital economic hearing was getting no media attention, and so no attention from committee members. One must have sympathy for the legislator, the politician, who knows that his bill, his issue, his candidacy may, for all practical purposes, not exist if it doesn't get on television. And so we are confronted with people desperately, or cleverly, waving their hands in our face for attention. And devoting an increasing amount of their productive time and energy to getting our attention.

No one is in a better position to manipulate television than the President of the United States. He can switch the State of the Union address from the traditional noon hour to prime time in the evening for greater political impact. He can demand time on short notice, and without giving a clear idea of the reason, which may or may not have to do with urgent national interest. He can time his televised news conferences for his own convenience, and can play the reporters present as straight men or persecutors.

One President built a career, and lost a career, on his ability at television manipulation. Richard Nixon was the victim of his own triumph in his 1952 Checkers speech, when he made an emotional appeal on television that saved his place on the Eisenhower ticket in the face of slush fund allegations. I believe this convinced him that he could always turn the country around by a television speech, and therefore failed to react in time to his eroding Watergate position. Concerned with image rather than reality, Nixon kept trying to alter the public perception. So his TV appearances came one after another . . . "A year of Watergate is enough!" . . . "I am not a crook!" . . . "Here are the tape transcripts that tell the whole story!" Right up to the eve of his resignation, Nixon seemed to be reaching out for that one great television coup that would galvanize his Silent Majority and halt the melancholy procession towards disaster.

If that massive effort at manipulation didn't work, it was obviously because the accumulating evidence of the tapes pried out by the Supreme Court, was too strong to be overcome by illusion-making. But it was also, I submit, because *manipulation* on television was being countered by *journalism* on television. Nixon's self-serving accounts were being subjected to searching questions, to outside investigation, and to analysis, instant and otherwise. That is why Nixon loved *television* as an instrument he could play on, and hated television *journalism*, which offered a disturbing counterpoint. It is why Nixon deployed his special counsel Charles Colson to pressure the networks into dropping "instant analysis." It was why Nixon used to tell his staff, "The press is the enemy."

So, it is my thesis that broadcast journalism is not only generally innocent of the charge of manipulation of the public, but, at its best, can serve as an antidote to some of the manipulation that is taking place. At its finest, it will puncture with fact some of the fantasies that the manipulators are weaving with greater and greater skill on television to beguile the public.

But, as television becomes an increasingly important—and perhaps today the crucial arena for most struggles—so the ranks of those who would use television expand.

Acts of violence seen on television—factual or fictitious—are sometimes emulated in a demonstrative manner. The Atlanta kidnapers of a newspaper editor sped with their hostage to a motel to see whether their act had made the evening news. A deranged murderer in California surrendered when he heard nothing about his deed on radio and television. For guerrilla groups, like the Symbionese Liberation Army in the Patricia Hearst kidnapping, manipulation of television is a central part of their planning. Israel asserts that Arab children are sent into demonstrations to draw fire, so that television will gain sympathy for their cause. Everybody wants to get on television, for some political or business reason. Or perhaps just to get attention.

I have a theory—which I hope to explore when I have the time—that television has become so pivotal in our society that some people are no longer sure they exist unless they can see themselves on television. For some, suffering a crisis of identity, television has become the arbiter of identity. So, they may resort to acts, violent or simply bizarre, to get TV attention and validate their existence. Television may have taught too well that the only important reality is the reality that the tube presents.

This, say the journalists old enough to have had pre-television news careers, this is a scary world we never made. We function within it and try to avoid being overwhelmed by it. We tell our stories through television, and try at the same time to resist some of television show-business values.

It is said that, as never before, Americans feel powerless, alienated and manipulated. And they see television as one of the villains. I hope they will come to see the journalists in television as their ally, not their enemy. We, too, often feel that efforts are being made to manipulate *us*, and, through us, the public. We will go on providing our antidotes in the form of facts and perspectives. Sometimes, the antidote may be information that has been stamped secret to keep it from getting into circulation. As the Watergate era has taught us, the "secret" stamp is a vital tool of the manipulators.

Sometimes, the job entails telling people what others don't want them to know—or even things they have been persuaded they don't want to know. If reporters had waited for popular demand, Watergate would never have been exposed.

To reveal what those in power don't want revealed, to tell the public what it may not wish to hear obviously entails some risks. Especially so in television-regulated, fretful, worried, wary of pressures from government and from local affiliates. But no one ever said that journalism had to be a risk-free profession. To those journalists trying to resist manipulation, in an age of manipulation, no one ever promised a rose garden.

A New Look at Journalistic Responsibility†

As a reporter, I hardly know how to respond to plaudits. We journalists lately have been getting more brickbats than bouquets. Perhaps I can take a leaf from the book of Henry Kissinger. When a woman came up to him at a reception and said, "Mr. Secretary, thank you for saving the world," he looked at her for the briefest moment and said, "You're welcome!"

Not many people say nice things to journalists any more. Jody Powell has just come out with a scorching book about the press, and he is only the latest press secretary to blame the press for most of what went wrong with his president's tenure.[1]

When the Reagan administration forgot to take reporters along on the invasion of Grenada, the press protested, but many Americans cheered. One wit said that on the next invasion, President Reagan will send reporters. *ONLY* REPORTERS! No soldiers!

What has gone off the tracks between Americans and their press? Why do juries sock us with big libel judgments? Why do so many groups resent us, from the left wing to the right wing; from Jesse Jackson to the Moral Majority, which, forgetting the Bible, will not forgive us our press passes? Why is "power of the news media" a synonym for manipulation of people where "power of the press" used to be a synonym for serving people?

One reason is the growth and pervasiveness of television. Television is coming to replace government as an authority figure and, therefore, a target of public resentment. The epithets once reserved for government—unresponsive, insensitive, arrogant—are now applied to the media. Many resent the influence of the media, which they perceive as more powerful, and more intrusive, than the government it professes to monitor.

The media are perceived as willing to sacrifice national security to ratings and circulation, and willing to intrude in private lives and personal tragedy in the search for audience-building titillation. I need mention only the reaction to the way some television people sought to

---

†.   This speech was first presented as the Remarks of Daniel Schorr on Receiving the Carr van Anda Award for Enduring Contributions to Journalism at the E.W. Scripps School of Journalism, University of Ohio, Athens, Ohio, May 3, 1984.
1.   *See* JODY POWELL, THE OTHER SIDE OF THE STORY (1984).

exploit the grief of next of kin informed of loved ones lost in the Beirut bombing.

Anchor persons for the big networks are perceived as overpaid superstars. Something went out of the perception of the reporter as a dedicated servant of the public with a press card in his greasy hat-band when word got out about million-dollar contracts for reading news from a teleprompter.

The media are perceived as powerful enough, and willful enough, to drive public servants from office and to spoil elections by their exit polls.

With the growth of television, journalism has become part of a vast entertainment industry, dragged along with entertainment in the fierce competition for ratings, influenced by television's addiction to drama and confrontation. Affected by the stage it shares, television news is tempted to see information in terms of conflict and to reduce a complex world to a simple parable.

Television news is driven to seek villains—a lot of them—and heroes—a few of them. The pursuit of stardom encourages some half-baked investigative reporting by video journalists nurtured on post-Watergate cynicism and looking for short-cuts to fame and fortune.

One ominous aspect of all this is the perverse incentive that television offers to the unstable and the fanatical. Because television goes to town on a hostage crisis, some are encouraged to plot hostage crises. The television movie *Special Bulletin*, about the nuclear explosion in Charleston, South Carolina, may have exaggerated the reciprocal manipulation between terror and television. But reality provides its own evidence of terrorist gangs that make media coverage an essential part of their plan—and find they can easily get it.

The Washington Monument siege in December 1982, was apparently staged as a media event. Norman Mayer made clear at the outset that it was the media, not the police he wanted to deal with. And he apparently spent part of his last day on earth watching, on a TV set in his van, the live coverage of his siege. Then he started moving towards the White House, to be met with a hail of police gunfire, at 7:30 PM . . . by coincidence, just as the network news ended.

Then there is John Hinckley Jr., addicted to movie and television violence, who set out to crash the media hall of fame by shooting President Reagan before the cameras. His first question to the Secret Service that evening was, "Is it on TV?" Hinckley may be legally insane, but he is not stupid. He wanted to get on television to prove he was a somebody. He surely succeeded. And television taught him how.

Why do I throw stones at the glass house I live in? Why do I, a reporter, criticize the news media? Because I fear that if we don't find the way to self-restraint, then others will find ways to restrain us.

I believe that news should be covered, but not exploited. A hostage incident should be reported, but not turned into a round-the-clock circus. I believe that we must learn again that people are persons, not generic footage. We must not trample on privacy, even if we risk losing a dramatic bit of tape.

We can no longer pretend that what we do doesn't matter. Television has profound effects on the lives of persons and on the life of the nation. It is the great arbiter of importance, even of identity. And now I am about to pronounce the ultimate heresy. Because this award ceremony is a special time for introspection let me tell you some thoughts that come to mind after the Jesse Jackson "Hymie" episode. Milton Coleman of the *Washington Post* had approached him about his problems with Jewish voters, and Jackson said, "Let's talk Black talk." Coleman later wrote, "I signaled him to go on." Coleman felt he had the right to use what he then heard as background. I don't second-guess him, but let me tell you of two experiences of my own in this ill-charted trouble zone between journalistic and other identities.

In 1957, working on a *CBS Reports* documentary in Poland, I came across Jewish families leaving a town with their possessions piled on carts, as in a scene from "Fiddler on the Roof." They explained in Yiddish that they were on their way to Israel. I had my camera crew film this unexpected vignette of post-Stalin Poland.

Returning to Warsaw, I asked the Israeli Minister whether there was some new policy that made this emigration possible. Staring at me in silence for a full half-minute, he said, "All right, I will tell you, and then you decide what you will do." (He could have said, "Let's talk Jewish talk.").

The diplomat explained that a delicate secret arrangement permitted Jews to be "repatriated" from the Soviet-annexed region of Poland with the understanding that they emigrate to Israel. But the Soviets, anxious not to offend the Arabs, had warned the Polish regime that the arrangement would be canceled the moment it became publicly known.

"So," he concluded, "your knowledge of Yiddish has enabled you to discover that Jews are leaving, and whether a few thousand more of these pitiful people can leave is in your hands."

I did not consult my superiors on the open telephone or cable to New York, but simply made my own decision to forget the story. Long after the fact, I told the episode and my decision, to Edward R. Murrow, who presided over *CBS Reports*. He listened thoughtfully and nodded his understanding.

The other episode that Coleman's experience brought back to mind happened even longer ago, in 1953.

Working in the Netherlands, I had learned of Queen Juliana's attachment to a faith healer. Under the influence of this strange woman, the Queen wrote pacifist and neutralist ideas into speeches planned for delivery on a state visit to the United States. The Dutch government, which was committed to the Atlantic Alliance, balked at the speeches. Unknown to the public, a constitutional crisis threatened.

I knew my way around the Netherlands and spoke its language. One of my stories had won the first William the Silent Prize for fostering Dutch-American understanding, and my reporting from flood-stricken south Holland in early 1953 had won me a royal decoration. So I had no trouble developing the story of the Queen and the faith healer from many sources—including the Queen's husband, Prince Bernhard, and the faith healer herself. After several months of investigation, I wrote a long article, which *Life* magazine accepted for publication.

The government undertook frantic measures to have it suppressed. I was summoned to the foreign ministry in The Hague and warned that publication would cost me all government contacts and possible expulsion from the country. I said that I would not be intimidated.

Then I met with a good friend outside the government, a noted historian named Lou de Jong. In a long colloquy, he undertook to dissuade me from publication. The government had been stupid to try intimidation, he said. The Queen's bizarre attachment, and the resulting conflict with her government, was a legitimate story, almost certain to come out eventually.

"But it cannot come from you," he added. "You are no ordinary foreign correspondent in the Netherlands. You are known, accepted and trusted. This story may deal a severe blow to our monarchy, and it would be too painful to have it come from you. You could not have gotten this story if people did not think they were talking to a family friend."

Dutch talk!

I agonized and temporized. I agreed to cable *Life* asking for postponement while I considered my course. Then the decision was taken out of my hands. Henry Luce gave orders to kill the article in response to an appeal from the Dutch government citing the danger of destabilization of a NATO ally. But I made no effort to have the article published elsewhere.

Three years later, the German magazine *Der Spiegel* broke the story. It was written in terms much less sympathetic to Queen Juliana's emotional problems than my article.

How do I justify killing two stories after a lifetime dedicated to "the people's right to know"? I have no answer, other than that a reporter cannot live by catch phrases alone. We have other connections. We have human responsibilities, which become greater as the power of our industry becomes greater.

I love being a reporter. I am proud that, in moments of crisis, like Watergate, when other institutions were muzzled, the press may have saved our democratic institutions. I have lived in too many countries, including totalitarian countries, not to appreciate how great our press is, with all its faults.

I believe that, if we are not to be vulnerable to demagogues who would limit our freedom, we must win back the confidence of the people. That means not overdramatizing what is already dramatic. It means respecting the privacy of the private. It means occasionally being willing to pass up a story if the human cost of that story is too high.

I thank you for this award, because I fear I'm about to be stripped of my press card.

The Press and National Security†

Had this conference been held fifty years ago, I would have appeared before you as one of the Jewish press. My first seven years in journalism, from 1934 to 1941, were spent in the Jewish Telegraphic Agency in New York. I worked as reporter, music columnist, national editor, and cable rewrite—simultaneously. In my spare time I wrote obituaries. The pay wasn't very good, but I covered a lot of banquets. Also, I got training in versatility and flexibility that would stand me in good stead, after shedding an U.S. Army uniform, in four decades of covering Europe and America for the *Christian Science Monitor*, the *New York Times*, CBS, CNN and, currently, National Public Radio.

As a long-time reporter in love with his profession, print and electronic, I come to you today aware that the press is under challenge. The last time I was in Jerusalem, in May of 1983, it was to participate in a conference on "The Media in Wars and Their Aftermaths." The unspoken subtitle was "Why do the media give Israel such a bum rap?" In the aftermath of the war in Lebanon, much of what was said from the Israeli side reflected outrage at perceived bias against Israel, particularly on the part of American television.

So, now, my subject is "The Press and National Security," and I know that many will translate this as "The Press *versus* National Security." I know that the American media are perceived as willing, and perhaps eager, to compromise the interests of the State from motives regarded, at best, as self-aggrandizement, at worst, as subversion. I am under no illusion that "The Press and National Security" is a dry, abstract subject—not in Israel, and not in America.

Let me first try to drain some of the emotion from the issue with a little historical perspective. Over the centuries, it strikes me, the role of the press in national security has gone through three phases.

Until the mid-eighteenth century, journalism was largely irrelevant to war and defense. Wars were conducted by kings and princes on limited battlefields with elite officers and mercenary soldiers. Public opinion was not a significant force, and the press was not a significant factor.

---

† This speech was first presented to the World Conference on Press and National Security, Jerusalem, Israel, Jan. 18, 1986.

In the second phase, the democratic revolutions had the effect of democratizing the battlefield. The need for popular support and popular armies established a relationship between warfare and public opinion. The press came to play an important role in enlisting and maintaining support. In the great wars of the first half of this century, in which millions were killed and many more millions were mobilized, the press was counted upon to help maintain morale.

For the most part, the press in most countries cooperated. In America, editors and journalists—one of them was Walter Lippman—were enlisted during the first World War to write propaganda. Official censorship was buttressed by self-censorship. The press was part of a national consensus. When the *New York Post* broke ranks to publish unsettling details of secret Allied treaties, it was condemned for that "unpatriotic" act by the *New York Times*.

The press joined in the mobilization campaigns. Journalist-historian Frank Cobb wrote that "there was no free play of public opinion" because "governments conscripted public opinion." That remained generally true of the second World War, of which Walter Lippman—this time not a government propagandist—later wrote that "the people were drugged by the propaganda which had aroused them to fight the war and, to endure its miseries." There is a price to pay for compliant press and controlled public opinion. One big story successfully suppressed was the Holocaust. As we have learned from belated research and disclosure, the massacres that Hitler was carrying out were no secret to the American and British Governments. But the Holocaust was kept secret in the name of the war effort. One British Foreign Office official argued, in September 1944, that to publicize the Holocaust would divert the Allies from the war effort and compel government officials "to waste a disproportionate amount of time in dealing with wailing Jews."

A change in press relationships with the national security establishment came after the second World War—not because of the scandal of the suppression of the Holocaust, but for other reasons. From reflex support, the attitude evolved into questioning and, finally, in some cases into an adversary position. At some point in the 1960s, the American Government began to find that the magic phrase "national security" no longer worked to guarantee a submissive and supportive press.

The breaking of the bond between press and government became dramatically evident during the Vietnam War, when official briefings were mocked as "the Five O'Clock Follies" and a conflict raged over "management of the news." But, before Vietnam, the assumption of omnipotence and omniscience had already come under strain in the MacArthur-Truman controversy over the conduct of the Korean War, in President Eisenhower's warning of the growing influence of a "military-industrial complex," and in the political divisions arising out of the Cold War with the Soviet Union.

Vietnam, compounded by Watergate, marked the final breach of the long-standing compact between press and state as the guardian of national security. Journalists, at first a few, and finally many, including even "Uncle" Walter Cronkite, questioned the viability and the purposes of the United States in Vietnam. In the Watergate scandal, it was discovered, the phrase "national security" was frequently invoked for purposes of cover-up. If protecting the state and its secrets had once been identified with the national interest, now the national interest seemed to dictate penetrating them.

Running parallel with press disillusionment was the development of television technology, and they combined into a potent force for undermining public support of the war. There was little about America's first "living room war" that inspired confidence in the living room about the rightness of this war.

Since then, in America, at least, the press is no longer the passive bystander and no longer the active cheerleader on issues of national security. It became the skeptic, the cynic, the relentless prober. The adversarial relationship cut both ways. As the press distributed the national security establishment, so the security establishment has come to distrust, and deeply resent, "the media," a term that sounds like a dirty word when used by some.

In 1961 and 1962, it took direct appeals from President Kennedy to persuade leading American newspapers to withhold details of planned actions in the Cuban Bay of Pigs invasion and the Cuban missile crisis. Today, it is doubtful that even a presidential appeal would always work. The *Washington Post* disclosed that Jordan's King Hussein had been on the CIA's payroll in the face of an appeal from President Carter.[1] Press leaks have exposed a CIA operation in Angola in 1975, and more recently a covert plan involving Libya's Colonel Khadaffi.

President Reagan says he is "up to his keister" in leaks. Inside the national security establishment the fury against the "media" is great. I

---

1. See, e.g., David Hoffman, *Bush and Hussein Longtime Friends; They Meet Today with Prospect of War Hanging Over the Mideast*, WASH. POST, Aug. 16, 1990, at A25.

have attended military press conferences that have turned into bitter confrontations. The professional officers, in particular, appear convinced that the press stabbed them in the back in Vietnam.

It was no accident that Pentagon professionals, with bitter memories, "neglected" to include the press in the first days of the invasion of Grenada. When the press complained, one officer said, "Next time, we'll send in reporters from the start—only reporters, no soldiers."

I do not know if the bond of confidence between the press and the national security establishment can be repaired. I do not think it will happen in the near future. Whether it should happen in the general interest is a matter worth discussing.

So far I have been talking about America, which I know a little about. In discussing Israel, which I know less about, it is important to be conscious of differences when one addresses national security.

One difference, again, is historical. The American system, founded on a certain distrust of government, emphasizes maximum freedom. Our constitutional assumption is that excessive secrecy leads to unaccountability and misuse of power, and thus the First Amendment is designed to insure that the press will be protected in exposing the secrets of government. Except in wartime, and with certain specific exceptions for nuclear information in peacetime, the government may not enforce prior restraint on the press—that is, prevent it from publishing something. There can be later penalties for publication, such as those which General Westmoreland and Ariel Sharon tried to exact.

Israel, as I understand it, has a totally different tradition. It was not hesitant, but eager to be a strong, unified state. From the British mandate it inherited a more restrictive approach to state secrets. No clear legal guidelines formally recognize the "people's right to know." Authority for censorship dates back to British emergency regulations issued in 1945. There are, I am told, provisions in the penal law dealing with official secrets. In this still very young state, the boundaries between the State's needs and the people's civil rights appear to be unresolved.

Theory aside, and perhaps more important, there is the difference between a superpower, with an enormous margin for error, and a small state, its back to the sea, in a constant state of siege, which does not perceive itself as able to afford the luxury of breaches of national security.

In America, the Nixon Administration claimed in 1971 that the publication of the "Pentagon Papers" on the Vietnam War would cause "irreparable damage" to national security.[2] The Court found otherwise.[3] Journalists may underestimate the harm that may be caused by unauthorized disclosure; officials surely tend to exaggerate it. It is my perhaps not unbiased belief that the real national interest in America has, on the whole, suffered more from excessive secrecy than from excessive disclosure.

I would not hazard a statement like that about Israel, where the stakes are higher and the possible damage from disclosure could be less theoretical. It is hard, however, for many Americans to understand the difference. When I asked an editor before leaving Washington what kind of stories he was interested in my doing while in Israel, his instant response was, "Israeli censorship. That's a fascinating story." It is fascinating because Americans find it hard to understand the predicament of a democratic state which finds it necessary to put limits on freedom in order to preserve its freedom.

It remains to be seen whether Israel, after Lebanon, will experience what America experienced after Vietnam—an erosion of confidence in the wisdom of the nation security establishment on which rests the consensus that undergirds cooperation between government and press.

Now for the tough question—Why do the American media "pick on Israel?" Why is so much made of the *Pollard* case?[4] Why did Sabra and Shatilla produce such a firestorm and the Syrian massacre of many thousands in Hana go virtually unnoticed? Why does American television make stars of hostage-holders like Naom Berri and the hostages who are manipulated mouthpieces for the terrorists? Why does television pursue relatives of hostages who predictably will put pressure on the American Government to yield to terrorist demands?

The answers to these questions involve the greatest current dangers to our common national security, for the news media are no longer a detached observer, but, willingly or not, an active participant in the new kind of war called terrorism.

The problem is not anti-Semitism or the influence of Arab oil money on the American media, as I have heard some suggest. It is the

---

2. *See* New York Times, Co. v. United States, 403 U.S. 713 (1971) (per curiam).

3. *Id.* at 713.

4. United States v. Pollard, 747 F. Supp. 797 (D.D.C. 1990). Mr. Pollard pled guilty to four counts of conspiracy to commit espionage.

nature of American television—its mindless love affair with violence, its elevation of emotion over thought, its tendency to change the real world into a synthetic world of heroes, villains and victims.

Now, this did not work badly for Israel in 1967, when this country emerged on the American screen as the gallant little David of the Six Day War. It has, on the whole, worked badly for Israel ever since then. It seems that, on the West Bank, no stone could go unthrown without being witnessed and magnified by American television. Edward Jay Epstein, in his book, *News from Nowhere*,[5] charted how the news that gets on television tends to depend on where television crews are stationed. And it had worked especially badly in Lebanon, where, in the nature of what makes Israel different from its Arab neighbors, it has been easier to make visual the violence that happens in areas under Israeli control.

The South African Government has reacted to the problem of adverse publicity in its own way. It has banned the witnessing of Black protest and the violent suppression of protest. American television executives protested mightily and said they would not allow this to affect their coverage. But the ban has worked. Last August the three American networks broadcast sixty-one stories from South Africa on their main evening newscasts. In November, the first month of the ban, the number had dropped to twenty-six despite increasing violence and fatalities. This visual medium has trouble conveying information without visuals.

The news media are today the arena of conflict, and American television, because of its competitiveness and dependence on dramatic pictures, is vulnerable to becoming the prize hostage. When violence is purposefully hidden, it hardly exists in television terms. When violence is purposefully displayed—because for terrorists that is the best way of terrorizing—it is eagerly accepted. Hostages may be paraded before the camera, offered for interviews or demonstratively killed as a way of getting attention. Indeed, State Department analysts believe that this is a reason for the increasing incidence of murders during hijacking episodes.

However the news is created and manipulated, television responds. Who would miss the chance for a spine-tingling interview with a hostage pilot as a gun is held to his head? If an episode of terrorism is big enough, the anchor superstars may come flying across the ocean, by their presence validating the importance of the story,

---

5. EDWARD JAY EPSTEIN, NEWS FROM NOWHERE (1973).

providing ego satisfaction to the terrorists and undoubtedly an incentive for new acts of terrorism.

The dirty little secret is the symbiotic relationship between television and terrorism. One need only be in a network newsroom when a hijacking incident occurs to sense the excitement and the heightened sense of being alive as forces are deployed, logistics organized and anchormen called back from lunch to pre-empt the soap operas and beat the competition with the quickest and the most dramatic coverage of a great story. At stake are the ratings on which the financial destiny of great media empires ride.

There is no villainy in this, only mindlessness and a reluctance of the media to come to terms with their influence and the perverse incentives they offer to the violence-prone.

If anyone should understand this phenomenon, it is President Reagan, who has been himself the victim of the rewards television offers to the violent. John Hinckley Jr., who shot the President, told examining psychiatrists that he had deliberately planned an assassination before the news cameras to win maximum media attention. Yet, the President plays his part on the media stage set by terrorism as he hints at forceful reprisals, challenges Khadaffi to meet him in some face-down in Washington and inflates the ego and prestige of a prime sponsor of terrorism.

The President would be better advised to use his immense popularity for a public appeal to television to exercise restraint in advertising terrorism—and then follow that advice himself.

Perhaps, we are all, in a sense, prisoners of the media age. But I would suggest that the question of "The Press and National Security" be reconsidered in the light of the contemporary situation. We can argue about leaks and censorship, but the most direct and immediate threat to our common national security comes from our inability so far to reverse the perverse incentives that television offers to terrorists.

The news of terrorism obviously must be reported. It need not be exploited, sensationalized. There should be no live interviews with those involved with terrorism. Anchorpersons should stay home in their anchor studios. Restraint should be used in reporting counter-terrorist preparations. (The day before I left Washington, Secretary of Defense Weinberger made a speech denouncing the media for reporting rumors of the deployment of a special Delta force unit at the time of the TWA hijacking.)[6]

---

6. *See* Phil McCombs, *TV Preview Terrorism: A Future of Fear?*, WASH. POST, June

Television has come, in some respects, to replace government as an authority figure. It confers identity and recognition. With that influence goes responsibility.

Vietnam produced a legacy of resentment of the press in America that we still cope with. It is my hope that television will act in time to avert a future wave of hostility on the charge of being an ally, unwilling or witless, of international terrorism.

6, 1985, *available in* 1985 WL 2110755.

Remarks on Receiving the First Amendment Award of the Ford Hall Forum[†]

I am grateful for this First Amendment award.

I will not say, like Jimmy Breslin, "Its about time!"

I will say however, that this award comes at a time that is important to me. This year I am marking my seventieth birthday and my first fifty years in journalism. Honoring me for service to journalism is like honoring a junkie for his drug addiction. But this is a moment for reflection.

The temptation is to make a long, rambling speech dwelling on remembrances of things past.

For example, May, 1948, when I did my first radio broadcast. I was a stringer in the Netherlands for ABC, along with a lot of newspapers and magazines. Churchill, Adenauer and other European leaders were meeting in a summit session in Amsterdam, and I was asked for a two-minute live report. Those were the days of squawky, fading shortwave communications, and it seemed touch-and-go whether I would get on the air at all. I heard myself introduced by the program anchor, did my two-minute report and, in the static-filled silence that followed, anxiously called, "Hello, New York!" to learn from the editor how I had done.

Briskly, he said, "Fine! You got off in time!" That was my first, and not last, lesson in what counts in electronic journalism.

Or I could mellowly reminisce about my first broadcast from Moscow, where I opened the CBS bureau in 1955. I was speaking from a glass-enclosed telephone booth in the Central Telegraph office. The acoustics were so awful that the technician in New York finally had me cover my head and the microphone with my fur-lined coat to eliminate some of the resonance. In total darkness, I found that I could not read my script, which the censor had cleared. For the benefit of the censor, listening on the circuit, I announced my plight and begged leave to ad lib, promising to remain within the limits of the approved script. I

---

†. This speech was first presented as Remarks on Receiving the First Amendment Award of the Ford Hall Forum, Boston, Massachusetts, May 11, 1986.

would like to think that the censor took pity on me. I did get on the air.

Or, I could tell you about my weirdest moment in television. That was in the Summer of 1973, during the CBS gavel-to-gavel coverage of the Senate Watergate hearings.

Handed the first list of the "top twenty" of President Nixon's enemies, I went on the air from outside the Senate Caucus Room, without time to scan the list in advance. At Number 14 I came to my own name, suppressed a gulp, and went on to the next names, which, as I recall, were, "Paul Newman, California," and "McGrory, Mary." The company was good, but the experience was surreal.

I could go on with anecdotes, and it might be the popular thing to do. But it would be wrong. Our business tonight is the First Amendment. The values that the First Amendment was written to safeguard are once again under attack, and, as the writers of our Constitution foresaw, from the government, which has seldom lived on easy terms with a free press.

One should make no mistake about the anti-press thrust of this administration, and not alone because President Reagan mumbles about "those sons of bitches" or complains about being up to his "keister" in leaks. In terms of trying to control and manipulate information, it is Nixon time revisited, but with more concentration and greater sophistication.

On February 23, 1973, President Nixon told John Dean, his words preserved for posterity on tape, "Well, one hell of a lot of people don't give one damn about the issue of suppression of the press, etcetera." (On another segment of tape, Nixon refers to me as "that son of a bitch." You see, presidential usage hasn't changed much in thirteen years.)

And so, Nixon deliberately set about driving a wedge between the press and "the Silent Majority." William Safire, then a White House speech writer, says, "I must have heard Richard Nixon say, 'The press is the enemy' a dozen times." Nixon had Patrick Buchanan write a vitriolic attack on the television networks, adding some tough lines of his own, commented, "This really flicks the scab off, doesn't it?" and gave it to Vice President Agnew to deliver in Des Moines. That was the famous speech assailing network news people as a "tiny and closed fraternity of privileged men, elected by no one and enjoying a monopoly (get it?) sanctioned and licensed by government."

Nixon wasn't anti-media, just anti-press. He liked television if he could have unhindered access to it without criticism or contradiction. And the same goes for the incumbent. Back in 1978, Ronald Reagan complained that President Carter had too much access to television.

He said that Carter was in a position to give America "a powerful dose of the presidency every week."

Well, no one has provided a more powerful dose of the presidency than Ronald Reagan, and, in 1982, he said in an interview with *TV Guide*, "I'm grateful for the time it has made available."

William Safire wrote in his revealing book, *Before the Fall*, that there was no doubt of a Nixon conspiracy to discredit the press.[1] Nor is there any doubt today. Anti-media sentiment is stimulated and exploited. More ways have been found to control information and more ways to intimidate those who might disclose it.

When things look bad, President Reagan often publicly blames the press. Questioned about budget plans that appeared to be in disarray, Reagan responded, "There is disarray approaching chaos in the press corps." When he came under criticism for his visit to Bitburg Cemetery in Germany, he accused the press of creating the issue. Blaming the messenger may come naturally, but it is also effective.

For, let us face it, many Americans consider the mass media too big, too manipulative, too arrogant, too insensitive: all the things they used to say about the government. There are a lot of people out there who don't like us and the Moral Majority will not forgive us our press passes.

When, in the name of "the public's right to know," the press protested at being excluded from the launching of the Grenada invasion, there was a dismaying scarcity of support from the public. One Pentagon officer, with bitter memories of the news media dating back to the Vietnam War, said, "Okay, next invasion, we send in the reporters. Only reporters—no soldiers."

In this climate, President Reagan finds that he can invoke national security to control the flow of information. In the war on leaks, lie detector tests have been instituted for Pentagon employees, and would have been made government-wide had Secretary of State Shultz not threatened to resign. Lifelong censorship has been instituted for officials handling sensitive information. More sweeping classification rules have vastly increased the amount of information locked away.

---

1. WILLIAM SAFIRE, BEFORE THE FALL: AN INSIDE VIEW OF THE PRE-WATERGATE WHITE HOUSE (1986).

The issue is not really leaks, but *who* leaks and for what purpose. David Stockman tells in his book that he got his job as Budget Director by getting columnist Robert Novak to write that there was a movement, which there wasn't, to have him appointed.[2] And, thereafter, says Stockman, at times of internecine conflict, "'going to war' meant it was time to call Bob Novak—the Prince of Darkness."[3] Three years ago the FBI was called in to investigate an alarming leak of word that Robert McFarlane, then on a mission to Lebanon, had recommended an American retaliatory strike. Three months later the investigation ended in the conclusion that the "leak" had been a White House background briefing.

It has been said that the ship of state is the only kind of ship that leaks mainly from the top. And no one has caused more agony in the intelligence community by compromising sensitive "sources and methods" than Mr. Keister himself—the President. It was President Reagan who, over Pentagon objections, used reconnaissance photographs for a show-and-tell on television about the military buildup in Nicaragua. It was Mr. Reagan, again, who, over the objections of the National Security Agency, had Ambassador Jeane Kirkpatrick play, in the United Nations Security Council, the tape of the intercepted voice of the Soviet pilot who shot down the Korean airliner.[4]

If President Reagan strikes out the "top secret" label because he has a point he wants to make, that is his constitutional right. But, in that atmosphere, how are others to know they are not supposed to use national secrets to make ideological points? A hapless Michael Pillsbury, Assistant Undersecretary of Defense, was fired recently.[5]

He had failed a lie detector test on a leak. The leak had to do with supplying Stinger anti-aircraft missiles to the Angolan rebels—a very hush-hush business, especially if the Stingers should fall into the hands of terrorists who shoot down an American airliner. So they made an example of Michael Pillsbury—leaking the fact that he had been fired for a leak.

---

2. DAVID STOCKMAN, THE TRIUMPH OF POLITICS: WHY THE REAGAN REVOLUTION FAILED (1986).

3. *Id.*

4. *See, e.g.,* SEYMOUR M. HERSCH, "THE TARGET IS DESTROYED:" WHAT REALLY HAPPENED TO FLIGHT 007 AND WHAT AMERICA KNEW ABOUT IT (1986).

5. *See* Dusko Doder, *Michael Pillsbury; The Agonies of Victory in Government's Substratum,* WASH. POST, Jan. 26, 1987, at A9.

How the Reagan Administration chooses to keep order in the government is one thing. But, apparently it also would like to keep order in the press.

I'll grant the State Department's Robert Oakley his free speech right to call NBC an "accomplice" of terrorists for taping an interview, at a place it promised not to disclose, with Abul Abass, wanted for organizing the hijacking of the Italian cruise ship *Achille Lauro*.[6] There is a real problem with such interviews—whether the perverse incentives offered to terrorists outweigh the news value of the interview. But it would be better if the controversy remained in the private sector rather than present the appearance of government pressure.

It is more sinister, however, when, as is apparently now happening, the government seeks to fashion a form of Official Secrets Act to control the press by applying new interpretations to old legislation.

This episode starts with a presidential indiscretion. In his April 14 speech announcing the bombing of Libya, Reagan dismayed intelligence officials by referring to three messages, obviously intercepted and decoded, that had passed between Tripoli and the Libyan mission in East Berlin. They apparently represented the "smoking gun" in the bombing of the West Berlin discotheque that was given as the immediate cause of the strike against Libya. Once the President had lifted the veil of secrecy, other details of the intercepted messages leaked, including direct quotations. Within days Libya was reported shopping for more secure communications equipment in Switzerland.

Nine days ago CIA Director William Casey met at the University Club in Washington, with Benjamin Bradlee, Executive Editor, and Leonard Downie, Managing Editor of the *Washington Post*. He was quoted as saying that, against the *Post*, the *Washington Times*, the *New York Times*, *Time* and *Newsweek*, the government had "five absolutely cold violations" of a 1950 statute that makes it a crime to disclose anything "concerning the communication intelligence activities" of the United States or of any foreign government if such disclosure is "prejudicial to the safety or interest of the United States."[7]

---

6. For a brief synpopsis of the 1985 hijacking, see Laura King, *Mastermind of Achille Lauro Hijacking a Force in Palestinian Politics,* S.F. CHRON., May 19, 1998, at A12.

7. *U.S. May Prosecute Paper, Magazine for News of Codes*, S.F. CHRON., May 7, 1986, *available in* 1986 WL 3738206, at *2.

Casey had apparently not informed the other publications of their jeopardy. His intention, it seemed, was to use the club of threatened prosecution for past stories to stop the *Washington Post* from publishing a prospective story dealing with the intelligence secrets that Ronald Pelton, former NSA employee, allegedly furnished the Russians. That the Russians already have the information may not be a defense, as Samuel Morrison, Navy intelligence analyst, found when convicted of espionage for having given a British magazine satellite photos of a Soviet aircraft carrier.

White House spokesman Larry Speakes seemed undisturbed about the idea of prosecuting a newspaper. "Anyone who violates the law should be prosecuted," he said. More alarmingly, Senator David Durenberger, Chairman of the Senate Intelligence Committee, and no friend of Casey, also seemed undisturbed. He said that leaks should be stopped at their source, but if that is not possible, it is right to go after a newspaper.

So, there we are. The First Amendment, which we honor tonight, says, "Congress shall make no law . . . abridging the freedom of the press."[8] But, Bill Casey and others in the administration say that we already have some laws that can be pressed into service. And there may be others. The 1971 decision of the Supreme Court, in the Pentagon Papers case, generally considered a victory for the press, hinged on the determination that the government had not demonstrated serious enough potential injury to warrant prior restraint.[9] Next time it may be different. *The Progressive* magazine was stopped by a federal district court from publishing a speculative article about the making of a hydrogen bomb under an interpretation of the 1947 Atomic Energy Act, whose sweep had not previously been realized.[10]

And now the Communications Intelligence Act,[11] which no one ever thought of using against a news organization, is being dusted off for purposes of intimidation, if not for purposes of prosecution.

Was Nixon right when he said, "One hell of a lot of people don't give one damn about the issue of the suppression of the press, etcetera?" We will get a chance to find out, and I am not overly

---

8.   U.S. CONST. amend. I.

9.   New York Times, Co. v. United States, 403 U.S. 713 (1971) (per curiam).

10.   *See* United States v. The Progressive, Inc., 467 F. Supp. 990 (W.D. Wis.) (1979).

11.   18 U.S.C. § 798 (1996).

sanguine about the short term, when the "sons of bitches" are up against the Great Communicator.

Yet, the First Amendment, almost two centuries old, has survived hard times before, and will survive hard times again. We take our free press for granted, and resent its sometimes mindless excesses, until something happens to quicken our value in preserving our free institutions. Such a time was Watergate, when the press helped to break the grip of a conspiracy in government. Such a time will come again.

There is something intoxicating, and ultimately corrupting, in the ability to woo a piece of metal called a camera and be rewarded with millions of dollars, or millions of votes. Dealing with the faithful by television is to deal with them by remote control, inducing a sense of invulnerability and cynicism that fosters risk-taking.

President Reagan shares much with evangelicals. They share the idea of big government as a moral evil. He has shared with some evangelicals the notion of a contemporary version of the biblical Armegeddon involving the Soviet Union as the anti-Christ. They share simple definitions of "good" and "bad" and a way of appealing to people which is basically anti-intellectual and rooted in a populist tradition.

In Jim Bakker's PTL[2] we see some of the pitfalls of charisma, when the laying on of hands was practiced in ways not quite prescribed in the good book. It is not coincidence that in the administration of the moralistic Ronald Reagan, we have seen more aides and friends of the President indicted, investigated, or convicted than in any recent administration. There have been more independent counsels (special prosecutors) named, including now one for Attorney General Edwin Meese, than in the whole previous history of the Ethics in Government Act.[3] And none of them—Mike Deaver and all the rest—appear to have lost the President's friendship. Under that mantle of the charismatic leader who doesn't like the government anyway, all things are possible.

But there is still greater peril in governance by charisma. It is the charismatic leader, reelected by a landslide, who comes to believe that he, and not Congress, mystically represents the people's will, and therefore feels entitled to arm the Nicaraguan Contras, or ship arms to Iran, by any means at hand.[4]

If you wonder how it could be that the President's high intentions could be carried out through a seedy network of arms traffickers and manipulative Iranians, it is because charisma sometimes leads to loss of contact with reality. Reagan aides were unbound by rules and

---

2. For a summary of the controversy surrounding Jim Bakker's Praise The Lord ("PTL"), see Richard Cohen, *Greedgate, Irangate, Godgate,* WASH. POST, Mar. 27, 1987, at A27.

3. The current version of the Ethics in Government Act can be found at 28 U.S.C. § 591 (1997).

4. *See, e.g.,* Edward T. Pound & Andy Pasztor, *The Iran-Contra Report: Reagan Administration Broke Laws in Pursuit of Secret Policy,* WALL ST. J., Nov. 19, 1987, *available in* 1987 WL WSJ295428.

institutions. All they had to guide them was the leader's wishes. "An anarchy held together by his charisma," in the words of Frances FitzGerald.

And, when, last November, word leaked out of Lebanon and the plot began to sicken, the President relied still on his charisma.[5] A well-crafted, well-delivered speech off the old teleprompter had always worked to turn things around before—after the bombing in Beirut, after Bitburg—so, why not now? But, the speech last November didn't work, and a news conference made things worse, and popularity ratings plummeted, and painfully the President became aware that the old black magic had lost its spell.

So, now, President Reagan gamely says he doesn't think he's been wounded, and refers to an old Scottish ballad about the warrior who says he'll lie down and rest and fight again. But, as usual, Reagan's research is incomplete. In the ballad, Lord Randall said that while he was dying.

In the twilight of charisma, we may see some positive developments. For example, the President has given indication that he is modifying his moralistic view of AIDS as God's punishment for homosexuals and drug users, and has begun to perceive AIDS as a public health problem.[6]

He is driving full-speed ahead for a meeting with Gorbachev in Washington this year, and Moscow next year, and his first arms control agreement.[7] Maybe it is a way of changing the subject, but it would be irony indeed if, out of arms for the Contras and arms for Iran, we got arms control with the Soviet Union.

This nation pays a continuing price for its over-concentration on personality. In the era of slick political commercials, media consultants, and processed double-talk in the guise of position papers, voters have found it almost impossible to discern what their candidates will do if elected. So they concentrate on what the media mainly focus on anyway—telltale signs of what candidates are *really* like, whatever that means. So, in a week, the breath of scandal knocks out the

---

5. *See id.*

6. *See* John E. Yang, *Bigger Battle Against AIDS Severely Hampered by Smaller Fights in Congress, Administration,* WALL ST. J., Dec. 28, 1987, *available in* 1987 WL WSJ291061.

7. *See* John Walcott & Gerald F. Seib, *U.S., Soviets Look to Summit with Optimism: Reagan, Gorbachev to Meet Amid High Expectations of New Era in Detente,* WALL ST. J., Dec. 7, 1987, *available in* 1987 WL WSJ293593.

Democratic front-runner, Gary Hart—Gary Hart, for all his "new ideas" and professional organization.[8]

In more mature democracies—and I use that word advisedly—leaders are chosen not by media plebiscite, but by parliamentary professionals. It may be, with the ripping of the charismatic veils from the evangelist in the pulpit and the evangelist in the White House, that Americans will awaken from the spell that makes them believe that the great father will solve their problems.

We have allowed ourselves to share a Reagan dream and substituted that for reality. It was a dream of morning in America and standing tall, gratefully embraced by Americans who wanted it to be that way and so were willing to believe it was that way. It is time to wake up to the reality of deficits, both fiscal and social, in our country and bewilderment around the world at where we stand on terrorism and nuclear armaments. (Think of it: the latest poll in West Germany shows Gorbachev more popular than Reagan.)[9]

Now comes the time to advise the young people who are about to go out into the world. My advice is: Don't go. No, I don't mean that. My advice is: Put not your trust in masters of the teleprompter. That is what have given us the charismatic leadership that has made America a nervous giant. Use the critical faculties that this great institution has fostered. Judge. Criticize. Don't expect miracles in public life. Don't expect miracle workers as leaders. When America has come to terms with the complexity of its problems and the fallibility of its leaders, then, at last, a nervous giant may become a mature, self-confident giant.

---

8. For a brief summary of the scandal that led Gary Hart to withdraw from the 1988 presidential campaign, see Paul Taylor, *Hart to Withdraw from Presidential Campaign,* WASH. POST, May 8, 1987, at A1.

9. *See* Keane Kirkpatrick, . . . *And the Two Reagans,* WASH. POST, June 15, 1987, at A13.

The Constitution and the White House: Freedom Versus Secrecy[†]

Having been indulgently told to make this paper personal rather than comprehensive, I start with Richard M. Nixon, who did me the honor of having me listed among the top twenty of his "enemies" and having the FBI investigate me, which assured me a place in his Bill of Impeachment for abuse of government agencies.[1]

President Nixon, his words preserved for posterity on tape, told John Dean on February 23, 1973, "Well, one hell of a lot of people don't give one damn about the issue of the suppression of the press, etcetera."

That may not have been a very inspiring civil libertarian statement, but it was a canny judgment. Public hostility to the news media was increasing and being deliberately stimulated. Witness the enormous success of Vice President Agnew's speech in Des Moines in November, 1969, attacking the television networks as "a tiny and closed fraternity of privileged men, elected by no one, and enjoying a monopoly sanctioned and licensed by government."

Nixon's hatred of the press is confirmed in recently-opened Presidential files. In a January 1970 memorandum to Chief of Staff H.R. Haldeman, he stated that the press should be treated with "courteous, cool contempt." Another memo, in January 1971, said that Nixon regretted having played the "good sport" at the annual White House correspondents' dinner, and that "treating them with considerably more contempt is in the long run a more productive policy."

An essential part of the Watergate cover-up was what Nixon speechwriter William Safire would later call "a conspiracy to discredit and malign the press."[2] In his revealing book, *Before the Fall*, Safire

---

†. This speech was originally prepared for a plenary session of the American Civil Liberties Union at the 1987 Biennial Conference at the University of Pennsylvania in Philadelphia, Pennsylvania, June 18-21, 1987.

1. *See* H.R. REP. NO. 93-1305, at 150-51 (1974) (section of the Articles of Impeachment entitled "Daniel Schorr FBI Investigation").

2. WILLIAM SAFIRE, BEFORE THE FALL: AN INSIDE VIEW OF THE PRE-WATERGATE WHITE HOUSE (1986).

wrote, "I must have heard Richard Nixon say 'the press is the enemy' a dozen times."[3]

That view is clearly shared by President Reagan, who has been heard to refer to reporters as "those sons of bitches." Habitually, he blames the press for his failures, most recently when he told foreign correspondents that the Iran-Contra scandal had damaged his credibility, not because of "anything that has been proven," but only because of the image created by the Washington press corps.

Starting where Nixon left off, President Reagan has presided over an anti-press conspiracy conducted in a climate, if anything, even more hospitable to an assault on the press in a time of polarization.

The competition for ratings in television has generated some intrusion on privacy and insensitivity to grief, such as the ambush interviews with relatives of victims of the Beirut bombings. There has been some exploitation of terrorist episodes. Network superstars are often perceived as more concerned about money and image than public enlightenment. Media moguls are seen as wielding too much influence on our national life. Chain ownership and the rise of national newspapers have tended to erode a sense of community connection. The public has, in a sense, transferred to the "big media" the epithets once reserved for "big government"—self-serving, arrogant and intrusive.

That is why Congress had reason to believe it was doing the popular thing when it wrote into law a version of the Fairness Doctrine, requiring broadcasters to cover community issues and to present differing views on controversial issues.[4] The bill was supported by a gamut that ran from Ralph Nader to Phyllis Schlafly. The measure was opposed by President Reagan not because he loves the "media" more but because he loves regulation less.

A distinction should be noted here. President Reagan's quarrel is not with "the media," but with "the press." Television has served him very well. In 1978, Reagan complained that President Carter had too much access to television, putting him in a position to give "a powerful dose of his presidency every night of this week." By 1982, President Reagan had other ideas about presidential television. He said in an interview with *TV Guide*, "I'm grateful for the time it has made available."

---

3. *Id.*
4. *See* Communications Act, 47 U.S.C. § 303 (Supp. III 1991).

Happy about his own ration of air time, the President was not happy with much else on television. He said there was too much sex and violence and, especially, too much traffic in "leaked" information.

"Up to my keister in leaks" has been the constant refrain from the White House. Presenting himself as the guardian of national security against an irresponsible press, Reagan has presided over the biggest chill on press freedom of any administration in my memory of fifty years in journalism.

New ways have been sought to suppress and inhibit the flow of information and more ways to intimidate those in government who possess information. The compendium is too long to deal with here, but let me tick off a few headlines:

- Efforts to tighten up provisions of the Freedom of Information Act,[5] expanding the exemptions and making it harder and more expensive to get information released. Happily, these efforts have so far not gotten very far in Congress.

- Attempts to force scientists and engineers to submit their defense-related research work for review and possible censorship.

- An Order (NSD 145) restricting the dissemination of unclassified information if deemed "sensitive." That directive carried the signature of Admiral John Poindexter, which helped to insure that Congress would force the Administration to back down on it.

- Repeated efforts to write a more restrictive Executive Order on national security information, tilting towards automatic classification and easier reclassification. Most of these efforts have been beaten back.

- An Executive Order (NSDD 84) exploiting the Supreme Court decision in the *Snepp* case[6] by requiring government employees with access to "sensitive compartmentalized information" to submit to lie detector tests in leak investigations and to accept lifetime censorship. Under a storm of protest, the Administration says it is holding these provisions "in abeyance," but they are still on the books.

- Unprecedented efforts to control the conduct not only of government employees, but of the press. Encouraged by the

---

5. 5 U.S.C. § 552 (1994).
6. Snepp v. United States, 444 U.S. 507 (1980) (per curiam).

October, 1984, conviction of Navy analyst Samuel Loring Morison for selling satellite photographs of a Soviet aircraft carrier to *Jane's Defense Weekly*, the Administration has undertaken to construct, from interpretations of existing anti-espionage legislation, a version of the British Official Secrets Act. It would establish a legal obligation on news organizations, on pain of prosecution, to suppress information that the government declares off limits under one or another statute.

Thus, Secretary of Defense Weinberger tried (unsuccessfully) to get the *Washington Post* to suppress a story about the secret military mission of a space shuttle flight.[7] CIA Director William Casey tried (successfully) to get the *Post* to censor a story about submarine tapping of underwater Soviet communications. Casey also warned Seymour Hersh (unsuccessfully) of possible prosecution for his book on the shooting down of the KAL airliner.[8]

Ironically, as intelligence professionals will tell you (anonymously), no one is more prone to playing fast and loose with sensitive secrets than Mr. Keister himself. The President ignored qualms about compromising "sources and methods" to show reconnaissance photos of installations in Nicaragua during a televised speech and to have Ambassador Jeane Kirkpatrick play for the United Nations Security Council a dramatic recording of the voice of the Soviet pilot who shot down the KAL plane. More recently, to justify the bombing of Libya, he revealed the National Security Agency's interception and decoding of Libyan communications with its East Berlin mission.

But President Reagan has good reason to bottle up the secrets that do not serve his purposes. Like Nixon, he has had some embarrassing secrets to keep. Reagan's information chilling, I must sorrowfully report, has been conducted with astonishing success. In a capital crawling with journalists, investigative and otherwise, the Administration managed, for more than two years, to keep secret the main elements of its Iranian and Contra dealings, known to an assortment of arms dealers, foreign governments and private Americans.

---

7. *See* Jeffrey T Richelson & William M. Arkin, *Spy Satellites: "Secret," But Much Is Known,* WASH. POST, Jan. 6, 1985, at C1.

8. *See* SEYMOUR M. HERSCH, "THE TARGET IS DESTROYED:" WHAT REALLY HAPPENED TO FLIGHT 007 AND WHAT AMERICA KNEW ABOUT IT (1986).

That scandal, for all we know, might be secret still had the Iranians not blown the whistle on the arms deal and the McFarlane trip to Tehran last November in the pages of a Beirut magazine and a speech by Parliament Speaker Rafsanjani. Then, in succession, there tumbled out revelations about the diversion of profits to Contra bank accounts and the whole gun-running, fund-raising conspiracy. As with Watergate, one stitch comes loose, and the whole thing starts to unravel.[9]

But, think of it! Here was the bite being put on Countries One through Five (plus the Sultan of Brunei, who, for $10 million, didn't seem to rate a number). Here was the Ollie North-Carl Channell "one-two punch" being delivered to rich conservative Americans. And Robert McFarlane was assuring Congress "with deep personal conviction" that nobody on his staff was violating "the letter or the spirit of the law," meaning the Boland Amendment.[10]

Think of it! Here was General Richard Secord, the patriot-profiteer of the private sector, sitting in on a White House session in January, 1986, while a presidential "finding" was being put together, blessing all Israeli arms shipments already made to Iran (including one with the illegal help of the CIA) and all of Secord's shipments to come, and a special blessing on the indefinite withholding of word of all of this from Congress.

Think of it! In November of last year, when the unraveling had already started, Poindexter, North and McFarlane were still concocting deceptive chronologies—a minimum one, a maximum one and an in-between one, to be served up to Congress.

The power of secrecy confers a special intoxication that creates a false sense of invulnerability, a belief that Congress and the public can be led around by the nose, forever if necessary. That it all collapsed is not surprising. More surprising is how long the conspiracy survived.

It appears that, for a long time, the press was variously lulled, intimidated or co-opted. When McFarlane and Poindexter tried, after the disastrous mission to Tehran in May, 1986, to put the manic Ollie North out to pasture, his job was saved for another five months by sympathetic columnists whom he got to defend his activities. Clearly, those journalists who knew what North was up to believed in it, and

---

9. *See, e.g.,* Edward T. Pound & Andy Pasztor, *The Iran-Contra Report: Reagan Administration Broke Laws in Pursuit of Secret Policy,* WALL ST. J., Nov. 19, 1987, *available in* 1987 WL WSJ295428.

10. Pub. L. No. 98-473, § 8066, 98 Stat. 1904, 1935 (1984).

those who didn't believe in it didn't get to know. And maybe some didn't try hard enough. In the end, as in Watergate, the nation escaped from tyranny and unaccountability by the skin of its teeth.

Brought home to us again is the wisdom of the framers of the Constitution, who created the First Amendment so that the government could not prevent the press from exposing the secrets of government. They must have understood how close is unchecked secrecy to madness. Whom the gods would destroy they first give "top secret" rubber stamps.

The lesson of two centuries is that we have, on the whole, suffered more grievously from excessive secrecy than from excessive disclosure. At this point should come an upbeat peroration about how we have learned our lesson and how, never again, will freedom yield to unaccountability. But, truth to tell, I have my doubts. I think the cliché I'm groping for is "eternal vigilance."

"Psst! Pass it On!"
Why are Journalists Spreading Rumors?[†]

In China today truth is called rumor. In America, rumor is elevated to truth.

Sources have always tried to manipulate reporters with rumors. Is the press becoming more susceptible to this manipulation?

Mark Goodwin's memorandum for the Republican National Committee, with its insinuations of sexual along with political deviancy on the part of House Speaker Tom Foley, was a great boon to the news media. It brought innuendo out of the closet. It enabled the press to rise up in indignation over the war rumors, blurring its own role in the guerrilla warfare that had preceded the memorandum.

The whispers about Foley were said to have started with supporters of Speaker Jim Wright, trying to save his foundering cause. Then they were taken up by Republicans, trying to parlay the Wright controversy into a clean sweep of the House Democratic leadership.

So it was that an unidentified aide to Republican Whip Newt Gingrich was quoted by the *New York Daily News* as saying, "We hear it's little boys."[1] So it was that the *New Republic*, relaying rumors about a "clean sweep," said they were supported by rumors of "sexual misconduct" on the part of Foley and Democratic Whip Tony Coelho.[2] When the weekend before the announcement of the Wright resignation, a TV anchorman asked a Capitol Hill correspondent whether Foley has a "problem," then one knew that a problem had been created for Foley.

Suzanne Garment, who is working on a book[3] about scandals in government, wrote in the *New York Times* that ethical attacks have become part of the standard armory of political warfare and that,

---

†. This article was originally published in modified form in FINELINE, Vol. 1 No. 4 (July 1989).

1. *See Spin Cycles: A Guide to Media Behavior in the Age of Newt,* WASH. POST, Feb. 26, 1995, (magazine) at W28 (quoting Lars-Erik Nelson's 1989 *New York Daily News* article).

2. *See* Larry J. Sabato, *The Smearing of Tom Foley,* ROLL CALL, July 22, 1991, at 1 (citing a *New Republic* article by Fred Barnes).

3. *See* SUZANNE GARMENT, SCANDAL: THE CULTURE OF MISTRUST IN AMERICAN POLITICS (1991).

correspondingly, the corruption story has become part of the standard repertory of journalists.[4]

That, however, does not mean that the press, in its competitive ardor for the next scandal, must become the tool of the manipulator. The question is not so much one of professional ethics as professional standards. It is true, and perhaps unavoidable, that private lives become public events in the age of Gary Hart and John Tower. We will do, and perhaps overdo, stories involving personal scandal. But one can ask that, at least, they be *stories* and not simply planted innuendoes, leers and whispers without substance.

It was understandable that, in the wake of the Wright controversy and the sudden resignation of Coelho, the press was in avid search of new names. But red flags should have gone up at CBS News when it was informed that Representative Bill Gray had been interviewed by FBI agents, said to be "involved" in an investigation of an unspecified subject. It really was not much of a story without knowing what was being investigated and whether Gray was a target. (He wasn't.)

Rita Braver, the able and energetic law correspondent at CBS, told me that her story was acquired by assiduous effort and was not a simple leak. I have no trouble accepting that. (She also told me, flatteringly, that she was only following my own investigative footsteps.) But I still think that the vague echo of a "preliminary investigation" was not a real story, that the existing situation should have dictated caution and that a more interesting story might be the one a reporter cannot tell—who broke the rules of confidentiality designed to protect citizens' rights?

The political war of rumor and innuendo is likely to go on, and the press is likely to go on covering and profiting from it. All one can hope is that the press will resist being enlisted as foot soldiers in that slimy war.

---

4. Suzanne Garment, *The Lynching Game—Washington-Style*, N.Y. TIMES, June 1, 1989, at A23.

The Real World—And Where Did It Go?[†]

Sorry to have been away so long, but glad to be back, and especially under circumstances less dramatic than last time.

Thirteen years ago I came here as a Regents Professor, for me a fancy name for a refugee. A refugee from televisionland after a bruising confrontation with Congress, which tried to make me reveal the source of a leaked confidential committee report. And, more painfully, a collision with CBS, my employer for a quarter-century.

It seemed, back then, a better idea for me to be setting in the West than trying to rise in the East. My quarter here with a graduate seminar was interesting. I tried to explain the trouble the world was in because of television. My students wanted to know about the trouble that I had been in and how close I had come to going to jail for contempt of Congress (which, you may be interested to know, is listed on the statute books as a crime).[1]

I wound up my teaching stint speaking at commencement on June 10, 1977, and headed for the airport and back East to find out if there could be life after CBS. There could be, and there was. A book,[2] a syndicated newspaper column, six years helping Ted Turner get Cable News Network started and, for the past five years, the quieter life (relatively speaking) of a news analyst at National Public Radio.

So now I'm back at Berkeley, having learned a lot more about the state of our profession and looking out at another class of eager young journalists ready to go out into the world. My simple advice: don't go. What they used to call the real world isn't real any more. It's become a world of sound bites and simulations.

No, do go. But be aware that we news people aren't as popular with Americans as we used to be. Journalism is on the defensive. "The people's right to know" rings hollow in a world of gossip and innuendo. Americans don't have the same warm feeling about multi-million-dollar blow-dried anchorpersons that they used to have about $150 a week reporters with press cards in their greasy hatbands. Many

---

†. This speech was originally presented as the Commencement Address at the Graduate School of Journalism, University of California, Berkeley, California, May 20, 1990.

1. *See* 2 U.S.C. § 192 (1996).
2. *See* DANIEL SCHORR, CLEARING THE AIR (1977).

of the epithets that people used to apply to Big Government—arrogant, insensitive, intrusive, self-serving—they now apply to the Big Media. People used to admire the "power of the press," a force for exposure of evil. They are likely to resent "the power of the media," regarded as a force for manipulation.

The great difference, of course, is television, which obliges journalism to perform on a corner of its entertainment stage, obeying the dictates of theater. You may be surprised to hear me say this, but television is not a very good medium for information. It appeals more to the senses than to the mind. It demands images, not thoughts. It is better at letting you share experience than comprehend experience. It pursues drama, confrontation and violence because these are what work best on television and help to improve ratings—which mean profits.

By rewarding violence, television encourages violence. It is the terrorist's friend, and they enjoy a symbiotic relationship. The militants who seized the American Embassy in Tehran in 1979, planning to stay a day or two, thrilled to learn of slogans on television like "America held hostage," and settled down for a run of 444 days. Terrorists have become as expert as American campaign consultants at the manipulation of television. ABC gets an exclusive interview with the captain of a hijacked TWA plane in his cockpit, gun to his head. NBC gets an exclusive interview with the hijacker of a cruise liner and conspires to hide his location. Television finds these terrorist publicity stunts irresistible.

On a small scale, I was part of that scene once. Covering civil rights in the 1960s, I found it easier to get on the *Evening News* with a Black militant threatening violence than with a moderate appealing for a Marshall Plan for the ghetto. So, I spent a lot of time interviewing Stokely Carmichael and H. Rap Brown. In 1968, a few months before his assassination, the Reverend Martin Luther King told me that non-violence in the civil rights community was in danger of losing out because networks, giving such exposure to irresponsible militants, were electing them as the leaders of the black movement.

When I first joined CBS in 1953 at the invitation of Edward R. Murrow, I had a newspaperman's misgivings about electronic journalism. So, I asked a producer what made for success in reporting for television. He said: "Sincerity—if you can fake that, you've got it made."

I remembered that when I saw the fake tears of William Hurt, in reaction shots shot after an interview that shocked Holly Hunter in *Broadcast News*.[3] I don't know why she was shocked. I can remember a lunch in Paris in 1962 with William Paley, the board chairman of CBS. He complimented me on a *CBS Reports* documentary on East Germany, climaxed by an interview with Communist Boss Walther Ulbricht. He had become enraged at some of my questions, stormed at me and then, incredibly, walked out of the room with the camera running. Paley said that what impressed him most was the way I sat there nodding coolly at Ulbricht while he yelled at me. I realized that the big boss of CBS didn't know about "reverses," reaction shots filmed later and edited into the interview, and I explained to him. "But, is that honest?" he asked. No, not honest, but routine in a medium whose heart is really in Hollywood. I used to wince when a director, asking me not to look directly at the camera would say, "cheat right" or "cheat left."

But, in recent times, "cheating" on television has reached new dimensions, not only altering reality, but threatening to blur a sense of what is real and what is fantasy. The three big networks, all subjects of takeovers by less tradition-bound management in recent years, are fighting for shares of a shrinking audience pie. And they are joined by syndicators who have found that made-up stories are more interesting and saleable than actuality. In the ratings war, reality is the first victim.

Do you think any more whether you are seeing a documentary or a docu-drama, an event or a simulation, a real thing or a graphic? Are people aware that recent history has not only been re-created, but revised in docu-dramas about the assassination of President Kennedy, the Watergate conspiracy and the Atlanta child murders?

Fakery has now invaded news programs, the last fortress of relative reality. What is one to think when ABC shows spy suspect Felix Bloch handing secrets to a KGB agent on a Vienna street on what looks like real FBI surveillance film? ABC apologized for not immediately labeling this as a simulation, but not for doing a simulation.

ABC's Felix Bloch has yet to be charged. NBC matched the ABC scoop with a spy scoop of its own—an Air Force captain in Berlin, suspected of selling secrets. He was never charged. And, to insure equal time for the networks, what is one to think of an exclusive report on CBS that Representative Bill Gray of Pennsylvania is under FBI

---

3. BROADCAST NEWS (Twentieth Century Fox 1987).

investigation, when it turns out that he has only been questioned in the investigation of somebody else?

The issue here is not so much professional ethics, but professional standards. How many ways can you find, in pursuing sensation, to confuse people about what is reality?

Here's another way. Three times in recent years I have been asked to appear in television commercials for large amounts of money. When I asked, "Why me—not very handsome, young or famous?" the answer was: a reputation for credibility. But lying for money would destroy that credibility. Another assault on reality.

The relentless erosion of reality on television has had a powerful ally in a president from movieland. Once asked what had been his greatest role, Ronald Reagan said, "President," and so it was. We awaken now to the mess a fantasy president left us. It wasn't true, as he told us, that you could cut taxes, boost defense spending and balance the budget by 1985. So now President Bush is so burdened with debt that he is hardly able to govern. Few noticed that Reagan tended to confuse movies with reality—his story of the heroic tailgunner posthumously awarded the Congressional Medal of Honor, the Nazi death camps he said he saw—but only saw in an army film in Hollywood. Few understood that when he said he would deregulate and get government off our backs, he was issuing an invitation to colossal financial scandals.

Ah, but he was great on television, directed by executive producer Michael Deaver. Give him a teleprompter or a few index cards. Put him in the Rose Garden or on the Normandy beaches, and he was an inspiration to behold—an inspiration, but unreal.

I believe that a blurred sense of reality is a disease that makes it hard to react to real events, real problems. I sense that television joins the real world with the athletic contests we see and makes the world seem like a spectator sport. I wonder whether this contributes to the low voter turnout at the polls, the low response to census-takers and the growing number of people who don't file income tax returns.

So, couch potatoes, wake up. The poverty and potholes are real and won't go away by themselves. The deficit is not a simulation. People dancing on the Berlin Wall made a pretty picture, but now there is Germany coming together.

So, get out there and fight fantasy, recapture reality. America needs you to resist a tidal wave of deceit and a mountain of manipulation. Your mission, the Class of 1990, should you choose to accept it, is to help bring America back from dreamland.

Confessions of a Journalist at 75[†]

It's very hard to be a hero in a room full of my own heroes and heroines. And I won't try. It's a wonderful evening and I've enjoyed it, but I did promise you something. I was so unwise, several months ago as to say, "Oh put down, as a topic, 'Confessions of a Journalist at 75,' and maybe by the time I get there I'll have some confessions."

The first confession I have to make is that I had marked out this afternoon to prepare this talk. But circumstances required that instead I would be involved in a two-hour call-in program on the hearings on confirmation of CIA Director Robert Gates. So I didn't get to prepare my speech. But, making a virtue of necessity, I'm glad to talk without great preparation, because part of what I want to talk about is my revulsion over the years against the homogenization and the packaging of information and personalities, to a point where one loses a sense of who a person is. There are too many organizations, there are too many consultants, there are too many speech writers. A famous television journalist writes his autobiography with the help of Peter Wyden.[1] A famous president, an education president, appears in a classroom, and turns junior high school students into props, while he reads a teleprompter. It must be a great education for young students to find out exactly how television is done.

After all these years I look back on all this and wonder what I can say that will bring us back to some semblance of reality. So let me make to you a couple of confessions, and maybe you'll learn a little bit about how I view a profession that is very, very dear to me, but part of an industry about which I've learned to have a great many reservations.

First confession: I actually never really intended to go into broadcasting at all. All my young life what I wanted was to be a newspaper reporter, especially a foreign correspondent, and most especially, a correspondent for the *New York Times*. Back in the very early 1950's I was a stringer for the *New York Times*, in Holland, writing assiduously. Finally, I went to New York, and said, "You know, I really want to be a staff correspondent for the *New York*

---

†. This speech was originally presented to the Smithsonian Institution, Washington, D.C., 1991.

1. DAN RATHER & PETER WYDEN, I REMEMBER: GROWING UP IN TEXAS (1992).

Times." The managing editor asked me to go through a trial period in New York to see whether I could cover local news as well as foreign news, and I did. Finally he said, "Go back to Holland. I think we're going to do it. It'll take a few weeks, maybe a couple of months and then we'll appoint you to our staff."

Time passed, and I wasn't appointed to the staff. In the midst of my waiting, there came this cable from this man, Edward R. Murrow, of CBS, for which I had done a few broadcasts. A cable I can remember as though it were yesterday. It said, "Would you at all consider joining the staff of CBS News with an initial assignment in Washington?"

Flattered though I was to be asked, I thought, well, this is radio, television. This is entertainment stuff. This isn't really for me. So I sent a cable to the *Times*, to Turner Catledge, the Managing Editor, and said I was wondering when this appointment was going to take place, because I'd had another offer which I might have difficulty refusing unless we could sort of settle a date. And, to my surprise, a cable came back saying, "We suggest you take this other offer."

So I said okay. And I joined the staff of CBS. A year or so later, visiting New York, I was invited to dinner by two editors of the *New York Times*: Emanuel Freedman, the Foreign Editor, and Ted Bernstein, Assistant Managing Editor. They said they had a confession to make to me. "You probably wonder why you didn't get the job on the *Times* that was promised to you. And I said, "Yes, in fact, I did wonder what had happened there." "Well, it's been weighing heavily on our consciences, and we've decided to tell you. What happened was that, just about the time you were to be appointed, the *Times* decided to freeze the hiring of Jews because, in case it became necessary to cover a Middle Eastern war, they had too many Jewish correspondents. That freeze lasted about six months, and during that time, your appointment came up. That is why you were not appointed to the *New York Times*."

And so that was how my career was shaped. So I went into broadcasting, with some reservations. I recall in the early days in Washington, I'd see my friend Scotty Reston and every few weeks he would say to me, "Had enough of broadcasting?" as if it was not a respectable place for a journalist to be. And I would say, "Well, not yet, but maybe soon." But I stayed with CBS for twenty-five years.

That leads to my second confession: Having looked with disdain that real newspaper-people had for this entertainment thing called radio and television, I began to enjoy it in part. And that bothered me. I recall asking a CBS producer for advice. I said, "Tell me, I can write a story, all right, but what is the secret of success for a journalist in television? I mean, how do you do it on television to make it work?" And he said, "The secret of success in television is sincerity. If you can fake that, you've got it made."

Well, I learned that lesson. And I began to see what he had meant. I began to see what you would later see in the motion picture, *Broadcast News*,[2] about the air-headed performer beating out the experienced journalist, knowing how to say, "It's grim, that's the way things are." To look exactly right, to look a little upset after a story about things one should be upset about.

You had to learn that in television a journalist occupies a very small corner of a very large entertainment stage. In this little corner you try to present a little bit of reality in a medium that doesn't welcome reality. A medium that requires you to present complex events in conflict, contradiction, good guys, bad guys. A medium where numbers don't work very well, where abstract ideas don't work very well, where philosophical ideas don't work very well. You have to learn to turn your little story about what is going on in the world in a way that will fit this very strange medium that doesn't like reality at all. If you add a little bit of unreality, it worked better.

Let me give you a concrete example. I went through all this business of learning about makeup. You had to learn about makeup because if you were out in the field there was nobody to make you up. You had to make sure you didn't have five o'clock shadow. That was okay. Camera angles, lighting techniques, all of that was part of this strange trade of journalism in television.

But then there were these other parts, these interesting parts. There's the part where you do an interview, and when the interview is all over, you turn the camera around to you and do reaction shots. Sometimes you repeat the questions into the camera—shorter, sharper, better than when you actually had asked them. Now you have complete control, and you are looking into the camera, and the interviewee is gone. Well, it was all part of the trade, and you learned it, and did it, and step by step you went along with it, and it was news on television. So what?

So one day in Paris, I and other CBS correspondents are at lunch with Mr. William S. Paley. The boss. The chairman. The man who

---

2.   BROADCAST NEWS (Twentieth Century Fox 1987).

owned this candy store. Shortly before that time I had done a documentary in East Germany. Soon after the Wall went up in 1961, we managed to get a camera crew in and spent the month roaming around East Germany for a *CBS Reports* program entitled, "East Germany: Land Beyond the Wall." The program ended with an interview with the then-communist boss Walter Ulbricht. He was not accustomed to being interviewed by an American. He took objection to some of my questions, became very angry, pointed his finger at me and shouted in German. Finally he yelled, "*Schluss, es ist beendet!*" ("The interview is over!") With the camera running, he walked out of the room, out of camera range. I thought that was a pretty terrific way of ending an interview with a communist boss.

Mr. Paley—I think now that he's dead I can call him Bill—Bill said, "That was a great documentary you did on East Germany, but let me tell you what impressed me most." I said, "What was that?" He said, "It was the way, as this guy, this communist in East Germany, was pointing at you and yelling at you, how you looked back, nodding at him in such a collected and serene way." I giggled, and said, "Mr. Paley, don't you understand what those shots were?" And he said, "No." "Well, you understand that when we interview, the camera is on the subject, and then, when it's all over, we turn the camera around and I do these reaction shots." And he said, "What are these 'reaction shots?'" I said, "Well, you know, first of all, we re-ask the questions so they can be edited in. Then for about 45 seconds I do a gamut of reactions." So he says, "Well, like what?" "Well, you know, like . . ." [Mr. Schorr demonstrates a variety of facial expressions.]

And he said, "So these things are cut in and they show you as giving a reaction that was not necessarily your reaction when this was going on?" I nodded and he said, "But is that honest?"

And he had me there. I said, "No, it isn't really honest. It may present a false impression of what's going on at a certain time. But it's routine procedure in a motion picture medium. Motion pictures require a variety of shots. The point is that we are trying to present a version of truth as done in this medium, which is *your* medium." With the luxury of two cameras some of the re-enactment could have been avoided.

This was his medium, and it bothered me that he said to me, "Is this honest?" In television news, a lot of things aren't honest. A person makes a speech in a crowded hall, camera people go up the aisle before the speech starts and get shots of individuals sitting there to be cut into the edited excerpts of the speech. They give you the impression that somebody is nodding approvingly in response to a certain statement. But that person has nodded a half-hour earlier, or an hour earlier, and may have reacted quite differently when the speaker made that point.

If you examine it, you begin to see that the fabric of television is a fabric of small deceptions, routine ways of putting things together so that they will run smoothly on television, a parable of reality. But illusion is what I worked with twenty-five years at CBS and another five or six years at CNN. That sense of illusion began to bother me. More and more I thought that our public, our people, our audience was losing a sense of the difference between illusion and reality. That has had an important psychic effect on society.

The blurring of the line between reality and fantasy goes further. The networks are in trouble. ABC, CBS, and NBC have all been subject to takeovers, creating a mountain of debt to be worked at the expense of less profitable operations. The network share of total audience is going down, and the broadcasters fight with increasing desperation for shares of a shrinking pie. They try to add excitement to the news. One way is to present so-called "reality-based" entertainment programs like *America's Most Wanted*. Reality-based, but unreal re-enactments.

Then there are the "docu-dramas," more drama than "docu." But docu-dramas seem more real and more immediate than the news. One docu-drama told the nation that the Atlanta child murders were not committed by the person convicted of them, and that he was framed. Another docu-drama told that Lee Harvey Oswald didn't really kill President Kennedy, and that he was also framed. In another, based on a novel by John Erlichman that represented his revenge against President Nixon, Watergate was presented as a matter of CIA directors, Richard Helms, and President Nixon blackmailing each other into silence. These things look like real news and real history. You talk to people who have seen them, and they all blur together, fantasy and reality. People don't know anymore for sure what is the reality.

And finally, the last barrier was breached, and re-enactment actually invaded a news program. July 29, 1989, was a watershed moment. ABC had a big scoop. Felix Bloch, American diplomat, was suspected of espionage. The ABC News showed Felix Bloch on a street in Vienna handing a briefcase to his Soviet spy. I looked at it and I said to my wife, "That's terrific. They not only have the story, but the actual surveillance film with the little clock running in the corner. Where did they get that?" Only later did they think to say that this wasn't real; it was a simulation using ABC News personnel. Actually, the facts they simulated turned out not to be correct, either. It wasn't in Vienna, it was in Paris. And it wasn't a briefcase, it was a suitcase. And it wasn't on the street, it was at a restaurant. And anyway, Felix Bloch has never been charged with anything. But if you watched television, he was convicted. Right away. And others have been "convicted" by the sheer impact of the way television tells a story.

NBC followed the ABC scoop a week later with its own spy scoop. Air Force Captain John Hirsch brought back from Berlin, suspected of selling secrets to the Russians. It turned out it was all a mistake. One wrong response on a lie-detector test. And the Air Force apologized, but not NBC. Hirsch is suing NBC for libel. But for the American public, John Hirsch was convicted. Such is the magic and the power of this medium that it can create its own realities and become, in a certain sense, more real than what we used to call reality.

Or—another scoop for NBC—a young naval petty officer, Clayton Hartwig. According to informed Navy sources cited by NBC, the explosion on the U.S.S. Iowa was probably caused by this guy who was having a homosexual relationship that had gone sour, and in revenge he blew up the ship. After two years of investigation it seems probable that the Iowa's explosion was an accident, but the story of Hartwig's sabotage remains a residual truth in the minds of thousands and thousands of Americans. "Oh we know what happened on the U.S.S. Iowa. That was that homosexual guy, wasn't it? He did that."

I have a small confession to make in that connection. I had vowed that I would not venture from reality more than necessary in TV news—that is, stay away from entertainment programs creating confusion about reality. But once, once, just once, I was asked if I would play a role in a CBS entertainment program called *You Are There*, hosted by Walter Cronkite. It recreated episodes in history using real correspondents interacting anachronistically with actors, as though they were there at the time. Interesting technique. I was invited to play reporter in one program. I asked, "Why me?" Because the program, called *The Zimmerman Telegram*, about an episode in First World War history, required a correspondent in Berlin. I was supposed to be at the Wilhelmstrasse, the German foreign ministry, and ask a question of the actor playing the foreign minister. "Why me?" "Because you've been our Berlin correspondent and that gives the thing credibility. Right?" Well, I did it. What did people who knew me from Berlin of the 1960's think when they saw me in Berlin in 1914 reporting for Walter Cronkite? As I say, this is a confession.

But I haven't told you my gravest confession of all. You will understand that I have the reporter's ethic—perhaps mystique—that I cannot stand in the way of information getting to the public. People can keep secrets, and, certainly, governments. But once I know, it's not a secret anymore. And then I cannot be the arbiter of what the public is allowed to know. In principle, I do not suppress news.

On one occasion, during Watergate, when I was getting a lot of exposure on CBS, a taxi driver taking me to the airport in New York turned around to me and said, "Mr. Schorr I've seen you on television. Why don't you tell us what's going on in Washington, what's really going on?" I said, "How do you mean, I really do my best?" And he said, "Nah, but you people know things, you know all these big shots and you're all in bed together, and there are things you don't tell us." I said, "Believe me, I'm not an insider, some people call me a quintessential outsider" (you might not think that looking at this audience tonight). But it always has been important to me that I don't decide what the public should know. If I know, then the public should know.

I acted on that premise in 1976, when I had a copy of a report that the House Intelligence Committee had drafted, but which the House of Representatives, in its wisdom, decided to suppress. It developed that I now had the only copy of this report in the "free world." I not only divulged its contents in stories on CBS, but then felt it was my duty to see that the whole report was published.[3] I got into a lot of trouble—and at one point faced the threat of being cited for contempt of Congress—because of my principle that I don't suppress news.

Yet, a couple of times in my life I did. I'm not sure yet that I did right, but I did it. I'll tell you one of those episodes.

In 1957 I was in Poland working on a documentary for the CBS *See It Now* program. In the course of wandering around Poland for a couple of months, I came to a place in Eastern Poland, a small town, where I saw an amazing sight. A bunch of people with horse-drawn carts on which their possessions were piled, like a scene from "Fiddler on the Roof." I went up to them, and soon realized that they were Jews. I didn't speak Polish, so I spoke to them in Yiddish, and they addressed me in Yiddish, and they explained to me that they were

---

3. *See, e.g.,* Matthew Yeomans, *The Voice Is Out There,* VILLIAGE VOICE, Nov. 14, 1995, at 32.

going to Israel. That was quite remarkable, because in 1957, Jews were not being allowed to leave Soviet bloc countries to go to Israel. So I did interviews with them on film in Yiddish—nice little vignettes to go in this documentary of Poland today after Stalin. But I needed to know how this had been arranged.

Returning to Warsaw, I asked the Israeli Minister how Jews were getting out of Poland to go to Israel. He asked, "How do know about that?" I said, "Well, I met some. I interviewed them." "Where?" he said. And I said, "Well in this town. In eastern Poland." He said, "Well, if you know that much, I'll tell you more, and then you can decide what you will do."

You see, the Soviet Union, at the end of the war, had occupied a part of Poland containing many Jews. They didn't want to stay there. And an arrangement was worked out among Israel, Poland and the Soviet Union. Jews there could be "repatriated" to Poland, with the understanding that they would almost immediately leave for Israel, because Poland didn't want them. The Soviets, worried about reactions among their Arab friends, had stipulated that if the arrangement became known, it would stop immediately. "So," said my Israeli Minister friend, "That's the story. If you want to go ahead, go ahead. But if you do, that's the end of Jews getting out of the Soviet Union." I said well, I'd have to see what I'd do about that.

This was all on 16 millimeter film, and we were shipping rolls of film every day to New York as part of this program that we would structure later. And I kept this roll of film there on my desk. I thought to call Murrow and see what he thought—couldn't call on an open telephone. And so the film remained with me in Poland. I didn't ship it. We finished the program, it went on the air. I came back to New York and saw Murrow, and said to him, "I think I've got to tell you something." And I told him that story. And he said, "I understand." Not quite approving. Not quite disapproving. Just saying, "I understand."

The Source of Evil and the Evil of Sources†

As text for this sermon I have chosen my favorite verse from the works of my unfavorite *New Yorker* writer, Janet Malcolm, "Every journalist who is not too stupid or too full of himself to notice what is going on knows that what he does is morally indefensible."[1]

She was talking about the cultivation of sources—specifically about how Joe McGinniss got Jeffrey MacDonald, the doctor convicted of murdering his wife and two daughters, to confide in him for the book *Fatal Vision*.[2] But, in generalizing about the journalist as a kind of "confidence man," preying on the people he deals with, Ms. Malcolm touched on a larger and troubling phenomenon of today— that Americans don't love us newspeople any more and will not forgive us our press passes.

In recent years a bias has developed that can only be called an anti-media cult. It turned out to be not just an aberration of Nixon times when Vice President Ted Agnew, in 1969, attacked television journalists in words penned by Pat Buchanan, as "a tiny and closed fraternity of privileged men," and drew down on the networks 150,000 messages applauding him. That distrust, approaching hostility, has grown. Political candidates have learned that the news media make good targets, and attacking the press has become a commonplace way to appeal to voters.

There are a lot of reasons for this. People do not have the same warm feeling about million-dollar blow-dried television anchorpersons that they used to have about $150-a-week reporters with press cards in their greasy hatbands. It's a long way from the reporter hero of *The Front Page*[3] to the depiction of our profession in *Network*,[4] *Absence of Malice*,[5] and *Broadcast News*.[6] The press is traditionally anti-establishment, but the media are viewed now as an establishment.

---

† This speech was first presented at the International Conference on Free Expression and Global Media at the National Press Club, Washington, D.C., Mar. 24, 1992.

1. *See* Linda Fibich, *Under Siege,* AM. JOURN. REV., Sept. 1995, at 16 (quoting Janet Malcolm from a 1989 article in the *New Yorker*).

2. JOE MCGINNIS, FATAL VISION (1989).

3. THE FRONT PAGE (Universal 1974).

4. NETWORK (United Artists 1976).

5. ABSENCE OF MALICE (Columbia Pictures 1981).

6. BROADCAST NEWS (Twentieth Century Fox 1987).

Epithets once applied to Big Government—arrogant, self-serving, intrusive, insensitive—are now applied to the Big Media. "Power of the press" used to imply a force for good. "Power of the media" connotes manipulation and exploitation.

We could live with unpopularity, but this hostility makes it harder for us to do our work. How far can we get arguing "the people's right to know" when the people are not sure they want to know from us? What good does it do to fight censorship in the Gulf War when opinion polls show most Americans want more censorship to keep us from spoiling the war and endangering their kinfolk? How can we win a fight for First Amendment privilege if people think we have too much privilege already?

"A tiny and closed fraternity of privileged men," said Agnew. *Privilege* is an interesting word. In its first dictionary meaning it is something enjoyed by the overly advantaged—like "the privileges of the wealthy." In its second meaning it refers to immunities of officials, "like executive privilege." You have to read way down before you arrive at privileges that are meant to serve our common liberties—like the privilege not to incriminate yourself, or the privilege to protect certain other confidences important to the community. The relationship between priest and penitent is privileged. The relationship between doctor and patient is privileged. The relationship between lawyer and client is privileged. That is because society, and the law, recognize that these institutions would not work without the ability to speak in confidence. And how about the First Amendment privilege that we claim—the confidential relationship between journalist and source? That rests on shakier legal ground.

So I became vividly aware in 1976 when I came before the House Ethics Committee. In its first mission it was trying to ascertain where I had gotten the draft report of a committee that had investigated the CIA and FBI. The House, in its wisdom, had voted to suppress the report, and now threatened to recommend that I be held in contempt of Congress with a possible long prison sentence, unless I disclosed my source.

My able lawyer, Joe Califano, and his associates had done their research thoroughly. The record of the Supreme Court reflected a disinclination to recognize any absolute privilege to protect sources when free press came up against fair trial. Furthermore, the record reflected a growing judicial hostility toward the press. The courts had given their blessing to police searches of newsrooms and enforcement of contempt orders for confidential notes and sources. In New Jersey,

District Court Judge Frederick Lacy had gratuitously described *New York Times* reporter Myron Farber as "standing on an altar of greed"[7] for resisting demands for his notes and sources. Chief Justice Warren Burger reportedly expressed his glee that Farber had gone to jail. In another case, involving a Boston bank, Justice Burger seized the opportunity to inveigh against "the modern media empires"[8] exercising an "unfair advantage"[9] in terms of "corporate domination of the political process."[10]

So, given the case history, the possibility that I would be held in contempt of Congress and go to jail seemed very real when I answered the subpoena of the House Ethics Committee. It did not help that I had become an easier target for the Committee when it became known that CBS and I were parting company. Became known, let me mention in passing, because Nina Totenberg broke the story on National Public Radio. She has never seen fit to tell me her CBS source.

Well, when I went up the steps of the House Rayburn Building on that drizzly September day, I was quite nervous. Speak of a "chilling effect"—I was chilled. And more so when Califano stopped on the steps and said, "There's something wrong with this whole picture." "What?" I asked. "Well," he said, "Isn't it always supposed to be the *Italian* gangster and the *Jewish* lawyer?" In the end, we won. The Ethics Committee backed off after the hearing—in part, I'm convinced, because Public Television came in at the last minute with one camera for a live telecast. I learned then what Ollie North learned later about the restraining influence of a camera on your tormentors.

So now its Nina's turn, and Tim Phelps, who broke the story about Anita Hill's complaint against Judge Clarence Thomas.[11] I have no inside knowledge of how far the Senate's counsel will go in trying to compel them to disclose their sources. Dan Rather said from this rostrum last week, "It's time we made some noise about them." And of course we will. An embarrassed Senate can only further embarrass itself by sending reporters to jail—as I know from expensive research, it has the legal power to do.[12]

---

7. Farber v. Job, 467 F. Supp. 163, 168 (D.N.J. 1978).

8. First Nat'l Bank v. Bellotti, 435 U.S. 765, 797 (1978).

9. *Id.* at 796.

10. *Id.* at 811.

11. *See* Lars-Erik Nelson, *Big Brother Reaches for the PBS Dial*, NEWSDAY, Feb. 7, 1995, at A20.

12. *See* 2 U.S.C. § 192 (1996).

But perhaps the time has come to say that the chances of avoiding and winning confrontations with government and the courts would be greater if the news media enjoyed more public confidence. It is America's respect for an institution that ultimately determines how much privilege it is accorded.

The approval rating for the news media is currently very low. People sense that news has come to be considered more as a commodity to be marketed than a mission to be fulfilled. The big networks have all been the object of corporate takeovers, and the new owners, saddled with mountains of debt, are looking more to the bottom line than high principle. In a climate of regulatory permissiveness, the obligation to perform "in the public interest, convenience and necessity" has become a dead letter. Fighting ever more fiercely for shares of a shrinking audience pie, media empires cut staffs and increase sensationalism.

The quest of sensation makes one vulnerable to manipulation by sources with their own axes to grind. Red flags should have gone up at CBS News in 1989 when "sources" in Dick Thornburgh's Justice Department leaked word that Representative Bill Gray from Thornburgh's state of Pennsylvania had been interviewed by FBI agents and was "involved" in an investigation. It turned out that he was not a target of that investigation.

In July, 1989, ABC broke the story of Felix Bloch, American diplomat under investigation—and presented a simulation, not immediately identified as such, of just how he did it. I don't know whose interest that leak served, but Bloch has yet to be charged with any crime.

NBC matched the ABC scoop with the story of Air Force Captain John Vladimir Hirsch, under investigation for espionage in Berlin. The Air Force found the investigation to be a mistake. Hersch is suing NBC for libel.

And finally, the leak to NBC of the Navy "investigative theory" that the explosion on the U.S.S. Iowa was caused not by accident or negligence, but sabotage by a petty officer seeking revenge for a homosexual affair that had gone sour. Since then the Navy has admitted it has no case and has apologized to the family of Clayton Hartwig. I am not aware of any apology from NBC.

We know how sources can exploit journalists. Remember when the *Wall Street Journal* in 1986 had it from authoritative sources that the Reagan Administration was mounting new action against Libya's

Colonel Khadaffi? Bernard Kalb resigned as Assistant Secretary of State when the *Washington Post* exposed Admiral John Poindexter's plan for "disinformation" in the American press. That was before Admiral Poindexter went on to greater things.

We have all been used by sources, including myself. And I bring this up not in criticism of colleagues, but as a reminder that the press is beleaguered and if we are to be accorded privilege, we'll have to be careful how we use it.

But let's not give up. We rise in support of Nina Totenberg and Tim Phelps and the others who may be threatened by demands to betray their sources. We must work at defending that precious privilege of providing information from those whose identities must be protected.

I believe still what I said before the House Ethics Committee some fifteen years ago—that when a source is betrayed, "the reporter and the news organization may be the immediate loser. . . . The ultimate losers would be the American people and their free institutions."

Spirit of 76[†]

Do not let the title of this talk, "Spirit of 76," mislead you into expecting a Fourth of July speech. Note the absence of an apostrophe before "76." I suspect that, even at this early stage of the presidential campaign, you may be already OD'ed on patriotic hyperbole. This is simply one of a series of birthday talks in the midst of what I consider my Aspen family. It is also a news junky's way of forcing himself to pause for a backward look in the hope of one day being able to kick the "what's new?" habit and begin to assemble my memoirs. So, last year "Confessions of a Journalist at 75." This year, "Spirit of 76."

Tonight I shall depart from a long-standing aversion to the cult of personality, that way we have of making political figures larger than life and historic forces smaller than life. Television, which I hold responsible for many deplorable things, has also contributed to overemphasis on charismatic individuals, who are pretty scarce anyway. In my television career I have, during political campaigns, avoided the candidate chase, preferring the pursuit of issues. I may be one of the few CBS corespondents who never aspired to cover the White House, preferring to deal with matters like health, education, civil rights . . . and Watergate, a story that did not emerge from the buttoned-up Nixon White House.

Yet there are things to learn from contact with the high and mighty—sometimes more high than mighty. I want to offer you tonight what is essentially a series of anecdotes that, for me, punctuate chapters in recent history and may help to illuminate present history.

First of all, Nikita Khrushchev, that earthy, ebullient, garrulous precursor of Mikhail Gorbachev. Like Gorbachev, he tried to save the communist system by softening some of its rougher edges. Like Gorbachev, he was the target of a coup by the entrenched forces that felt threatened by him.

But in the fall of 1955, when I opened the CBS News bureau in Moscow, Khrushchev was on the rise, traveling widely, including to America, and accessible in Moscow as the fast-talking salesman for a failing system. He set unreachable goals of overtaking and surpassing America. He brandished missiles and sputniks to hide the inner rot in

---

†. This speech was originally presented at the Paepcke Auditorium, Aspen Institute for Humanistic Studies, Aspen, Colorado, Aug. 27, 1992.

the civilian economy. He was more successful in launching orbiting earth satellites in space than keeping Soviet satellites in orbit on earth.

I covered him in Moscow and abroad as a sort of Kremlin counterpart of a White House correspondent. He became so used to seeing me in his wake that once, when I caught up to him on a trip up a mountain in Austria, he pointed to me, "Here comes my Sputnik!" My exertions paid off in a first-ever television interview—an hour-long appearance from the Kremlin on the CBS *Face the Nation* program. But banter with the boss of the Kremlin didn't always pay off.

In October, 1956, Khrushchev returned to Moscow from an unusually long vacation, facing ferment in Poland, an anti-communist revolution in Hungary and a war in the Middle East over the Suez Canal. We correspondents heard rumors, which no one in authority would discuss, of an emergency meeting of the Communist Party Central Committee to make some drastic decisions.

At a diplomatic reception I engaged Khrushchev in discussion about his hunting trip with Marshal Tito in the Crimea, then asked if I could take such a trip. "*Pozhalusta!*" he bellowed, "of course you can." But I said I had a problem—my capitalist bosses back in New York would not let me leave on vacation as long as an important Central Committee meeting was a possibility. Discerning the direction of the conversation, Khrushchev bent towards me, lowered his voice and asked when I wanted to go and for how long. "Tomorrow . . . or two weeks." In a whisper he said, "Correspondent Schorr, you can go on the trip." I whispered back, "You mean . . . no Central Committee meeting?" "No," he whispered, "If absolutely necessary, we will have the meeting without you."

They don't make them like that any more.

P.S.　　The Central Committee met. Soon the tanks rolled into Hungary to crush the uprising. An invasion of Poland was narrowly averted. Poland's communist chief, Wladyslaw Gomulka, once a prisoner of Stalin, came to Moscow. Khrushchev trying to hold his empire together, made a table-thumping speech at a Polish reception, proclaiming the victory of communism over capitalism, and saying the words that would come back to haunt him, "We will bury you!"

P.P.S.　　I was briefly arrested by the KGB on trumped-up charges and barred from the Soviet Union at the end of 1957. Three decades later I returned to cover the Reagan-Gorbachev summit. I took time out to visit the cemetery (not the Kremlin wall) where Khrushchev is buried. Before his stark black and white tombstone I said, to no one in particular, "So, Nikita Sergeevich, in the end they buried *you*."

Richard Nixon . . . I don't know how I came to qualify for his Enemies List. I do know that the most startling experience of my career was being handed the list of twenty while I was live on television from the Senate Watergate hearings, reading the names aloud and almost choking when I came to my own name at Number 14. What I did to make that honor roll, I do not know, but I do know why President Nixon had the FBI investigate me in 1971.

On the *CBS Evening News* I had given an unfavorable review to a Nixon speech to the Knights of Columbus promising aid to parochial schools that, given Supreme Court rulings, seemed no more than political rhetoric. The writer of that speech, Patrick Buchanan, lovable then as now, called me to the White House to upbraid me and, beknownst to me at the time, suggested to the President that J. Edgar Hoover be asked to look into my background.

Hoover, apparently misconstruing the request, launched a wide-open routine "background check" of the kind that is preliminary to presidential appointment, including an interview with me. The White House abruptly called off the investigation and started working on a cover story. This was Watergate in miniature ten months before Watergate. White House Personnel Director Fred Malek was asked to identify the job for which I could theoretically have been considered, and when the story of the investigation broke in the *Washington Post*, press spokesman Ron Ziegler was ready with the deadpan explanation that I had been considered for a public information post in the Council on Environmental Quality, but, because of a slip-up, had not been informed. Not many believed that story.

Eventually the President's men had to confess all, under oath before the Senate Watergate Committee and the House Judiciary Committee, which conducted impeachment proceedings against President Nixon. One of three counts in the Bill of Impeachment was "Abuse of government agencies," and under that the specification was Nixon's use of the FBI for an unwarranted investigation of a journalist.[1]

So, now the P.S. A few months ago I saw Nixon to talk to for the first time since his resignation in 1974. It was at a dinner meeting where he reported on a trip to the former Soviet Union. At the end I

---

1. *See* H.R. REP. No. 93-1305, at 150-51 (1974) (section of the Articles of Impeachment entitled "Daniel Schorr FBI Investigation").

could not restrain myself from going up to greet him. As I began to re-introduce myself, he interrupted, "Dan Schorr. Glad to see you. Damn near hired you once."

Since then I have had occasion to break a story about a memorandum that Nixon circulated, criticizing President Bush for missing the boat on aid to Russia. And I have interviewed Nixon for National Public Radio. Campaigning for ex-President, Nixon seems no longer to have an Enemies List. I never had one.

Gerald Ford, our unelected President. . . . His problem with me stemmed from the fact that he had to deal with a legacy of CIA and FBI abuses that came under investigation in the wake of Watergate, and I was assigned by CBS to cover this son of Watergate. I embarrassed Ford by reporting an indiscretion of his that led to the revelation of one of the CIA's darkest secrets—its involvement in assassination conspiracies against Fidel Castro and other Third World figures unpopular with various presidents going back to Eisenhower. (No one, incidentally, was ever actually assassinated, but not for want of trying.)

The way the disclosure came about was that President Ford had received from CIA Director William Colby a secret report on past abuses and improprieties. With this in mind he told the publisher and editors of the *New York Times* at a White House luncheon that he had to be careful about who was allowed to search through agency records because they might trip over matters much worse than what was being currently investigated. "Like what," asked the irrepressible editor, A.M. Rosenthal. "Like assassinations," President Ford fired back impulsively, and then asked that those present forget what he had said. Publisher "Punch" Sulzberger, over the objection of some of his staff, agreed to keep it off the record. Word of the luncheon eventually reached me. I got Director Colby to confirm there had been assassination plots, and broke the story, including reference to the Ford indiscretion, on the *CBS Evening News*. That led the Senate Intelligence Committee, under Frank Church, to launch a special investigation.

Once again I got into President Ford's hair, figuratively speaking, when the House Intelligence Committee compiled a report on CIA failures and improprieties, including the betrayal of the Kurds in Iraq. The Ford Administration managed to persuade the House to vote two to one to suppress the report on national security grounds. I, having obtained an advance draft, reported its contents extensively on CBS, then made the whole report available for publication in the *Village*

Voice.[2] President Ford and Secretary Kissinger denounced the leak. That was in 1976.

Fast forward to 1992. I don't know what to make of it that Larry Buendorf, the long-time chief of the Secret Service detail protecting Ford (he still has Secret Service protection) has filed a $1.1 million libel suit against me, Scott Simon and National Public Radio. At issue is a discussion I had last April with Scott on *Weekend Edition Saturday.* Troubled by the revelation in *USA Today* that Arthur Ashe is suffering from AIDS, I made the point that the media should be more sensitive to privacy rights, even of well-known people. As a case in point I cited the person who helped to foil an attempt on the life of President Ford in 1975, only to be later identified in the press as a homosexual.

Having forgotten that there were two attempts on Ford's life in the same month—one in San Francisco, one in Sacramento—I confused the two episodes and named Buendorf as the homosexual, when I should have named Oliver Sipple, who has since died.

Had Buendorf called the error to my attention, I would have broadcast an immediate correction and apology. But I never heard from him. Instead, almost four months later, with no advance notice, he filed his action in Federal District Court in Washington. I then broadcast the apology I would have been glad to make last April. I am left wondering why the special agent of the Secret Service who helped to save President Ford's life seventeen years ago and guards him still in his Vail and Palm Springs residences would choose to make a Federal case out of a mistake—dumb, but not malicious.

Finally, a personal experience with George Bush, who seems to display a multiple personality in public. In victory, kinder and gentler. In the primary, caring. In the general election campaign, the fierce warrior, something between Rambo and Truman. (Although I don't think that Truman, son of a poor Missouri farmer, without a college education, a failed haberdasher, would recognize any kinship with a patrician Yalie petroleum millionaire.)

But, before he fell into the hands of the handlers and image-makers, there was a genuine Bush, obedient servant of Presidents Nixon, Ford and Reagan in a wide variety of positions, a person of engaging warmth and civility, friendly with Congress and the press that he now bashes.

---

2. *See* Matthew Yeomans, *The Voice Is Out There,* VILLIAGE VOICE, Nov. 14, 1995, at 32.

I remember a nice thing he did as CIA Director in 1976, when I was a controversial journalist. The *Washington Star* published a front-page picture of Bush talking to me on Capitol Hill, with a caption suggesting that we were having an argument, which we weren't at all. Bush called me at home saying that he wanted to apologize if he had caused me any embarrassment. That was a nice gesture, especially since we were dining that evening at the same embassy, and a very worried ambassador needed to be reassured that there would be no incident.

So there is no animus in the story I am about to tell because it told me something about George Bush. The only white tie affair I have ever attended in Washington is the Gridiron dinner, and since the white tie invitation calls for "full decorations," and I happen to have a couple of them—from the Netherlands and Germany—I decided in 1983 to go in full gaudy regalia. Dangling on my chest the red-black German Grand Cross of Merit. Dripping from my lapel the orange-and-blue Order of Orange-Nassau.

In the middle of a crowd of a couple thousand during the pre-dinner reception, I saw Vice President and Barbara Bush headed my way. Bush greeted me and asked, "What's that you're wearing?" I began to explain about the decorations, when he turned to his wife and said, "Barbara, why don't I have any of those?" I broke the embarrassed silence that followed by venturing that I vaguely recalled something in the Constitution that barred foreign decorations for Federal officers—something about emoluments and titles of nobility.[3] Bush turned to his wife again and said, "Then how come George Shultz has that ribbon in his buttonhole?" She explained that maybe Secretary Shultz had gotten that (the French Legion of Honor) when he was out of government in the Bechtel Corporation. The Vice President turned back to me and asked if I was sure about the constitutional ban, and I promised to look it up for him, which I did, and sent him a photocopy of a page of the constitution he had sworn to uphold. And he thanked me with a warm hand-written note that said I had eased his mind considerably.

Decide for yourself what that story tells about the breadth of vision of the leader of the Free World—the leader of the *whole* world.

---

3.   *See* U.S. Const. art. I, § 9, cl. 8 (". . . no Persons holding any Office of Profit or Trust under them shall, without the Consent of the Congress, accept of any present, Emolument, Office, or Title, of any kind whatever, from any King, Prince, or foreign State.").

From this and the other anecdotes, I have no sweeping conclusions to offer you about the nature or contemporary leadership. At seventy-six, I feel more tentative about these things than I did at twenty-six.

But when I was twenty-six, there was no television. And I do sense that made-for-television politicians are different from pre-television politicians. They tend to become programmed for television programs, and, in the process, lose some of their originality, perhaps some of their souls.

When you meet some of them close up, in informal or unguarded moments, as my profession has enabled me to do, you are sometimes surprised at what commonplace characters they can be off camera. Lives of great men oft remind us, as Longfellow never said, that no man is a hero to his valet, and few are heroes to us journalists.

The Trouble with Television: Biting the Hand That Fed Me†

This is the third in a series of annual pre-birthday talks in Aspen that I think of as memos to myself in preparation for writing my memoirs. Two years ago the title was, "Confessions of a Journalist at 75." Last year it was, "Spirit of 76." This time, because "77" is a neither here nor there number, the title is, "The Trouble with Television: Biting the Hand that Fed Me."

Why would I want to do that? I had twenty-three rewarding years with CBS News as a correspondent at home and abroad and six years with Ted Turner and the Cable News Network. And, if both associations ended with blow-ups over what I considered issues of principle, I harbor no hard feelings. I have extended general amnesty to Bill Paley, whose memorial service I attended, and to Ted Turner, as, indeed, to all of those with whom I crossed swords in stressful times—even Richard Nixon.

My problem with television goes beyond my own relations with the medium although my experience in television gave me a special sensitivity to its baneful effects on the American psyche. Let me put it in a sound-bite for those who have early dinner plans: Television, by celebrating violence, promotes violence. By rewarding terrorism, it encourages terrorism. By trivializing great issues, it buries great issues. By blurring the line between fantasy and reality, it crowds out reality.

And people are beginning to catch on. I do not know why it is that conservatives seem generally more concerned about sex on television and liberals more concerned about violence on television. The Christian Right is appalled at the number of sex scenes. Of forty-five such scenes watched by *USA Today* in a sample week, only four involved married couples, thirty-nine involved adulterers or unmarried persons and, apparently, nobody using condoms.[1] Others are more appalled by violence. By the age of eighteen, according to the National

---

†. This speech was originally presented at the Paepcke Auditorium, Aspen Institute for Humanistic Studies, Aspen, Colorado, Aug. 19, 1993.

1. Barbara Hansen & Carol Knopes, *TV vs. Reality*, USA TODAY, July 6, 1993, at 1A.

Coalition on Television Violence, the average American will have witnessed 200,000 acts of violence, including 40,000 murders.[2]

Pope John Paul seemed surprised at the thunderous applause he got when he told a Denver audience that the media must accept some part of the responsibility for the epidemic of killings sweeping across this country. Like the practiced orator he is, the Pontiff stuck with the theme and ad-libbed a couple more lines. "I repeat once more, including the media . . . Who is responsible for the media?" And many in the crowd responded, "We are."

The Pope shouldn't have been surprised at the heartfelt response. Opinion polls indicate that up to eighty percent of Americans today think there is too much violence on television. I wish that, while in Denver, the Pope had had time to learn about a young man from nearby Evergreen named John Hinckley, Jr.

"In the absence of family, peer, and school relationships," said the 1969 National Commission on Violence, "television becomes the most compatible substitute for real life experience." John Hinckley was one of those. He withdrew from school and family life and retreated into a world of fantasy violence, spending many hours alone in a room with a television set, eating junk food. In the movies, and on television, he saw the film *Taxi Driver*,[3] about a psychopath whose search for identity led him to try to kill a presidential candidate, hoping thus to impress a woman who had shown no interest in him.

John Hinckley wanted to impress the actress, Jodie Foster. So, on March 30, 1981, the disturbed young man shot President Reagan in the presence of the cameras which, since the assassination of President Kennedy, have always been around the President in case something should happen to him. And, questioned that evening by the Secret Service, Hinckley's first question was, "Is it on TV?" Transported to courtrooms in helicopters and police-escorted limousines, he wrote, "I feel like the President now, with my own retinue. We both wear bullet-proof vests now."

Crazy, but not stupid. Hinckley had learned the important lesson that television is the arbiter of identity, and he had achieved identity by a spectacular act of violence of the kind that television celebrates. Jodie Foster was still not impressed, but a lot of other people were. In the ensuing days the Secret Service received hundreds of telephone

---

2. Christopher Lee Philips, *Task Force on TV Violence*, BROADCASTING & CABLE, June 14, 1993, at 69.

3. TAXI DRIVER (Columbia Pictures 1976).

tips about persons talking of killing the President. One came from New York to fulfill Hinckley's mission, as he put it, and was arrested.

Anyone who has worked in television knows of its power to create a reality of its own that may crowd out *real* reality. When I was no longer regularly on television, a stranger stopped me in a restaurant and asked, "Didn't you used to be Daniel Schorr?" That is one of the more benign effects of television. Less benign is what people will sometimes do to get themselves and their causes authenticated by television. Prison rioters sometimes list as a primary demand that they be able to air their grievances on television. Anybody here old enough to remember 1977 will recall when Anthony George Kiritsis in Indianapolis wired a sawed-off shotgun to the neck of a hostage, led him out in front of the police and the TV cameras and yelled, "Get those cameras on! I'm a goddamn national hero!"

You may say that television is the victim, not the instigator of terrorism. But the dirty little secret is that television enjoys the visceral tingle of a terrorist incident, and enjoys more the ratings—and therefore profits—that go with televised terror. ABC scored an exclusive interview with the captain of a hijacked TWA plane in Lebanon, who spoke with a captor's gun to his head. A triumph for ABC—and a triumph for the terrorists who gained international recognition by this promotional stunt. NBC had an exclusive interview with Abul Abass, wanted for murder in the hijacking of the cruise ship *Achille Lauro*,[4] and agreed not to reveal where it had interviewed the fugitive, who used his opportunity to justify terrorism on American TV. Anthony Quainton, who used to head the State Department's Office for Combating Terrorism, has associated the increase in casualties during hijackings and hostage-takings during the 1980s with a desire to insure media attention.

Television has offered incentives not only for destructive behavior, but for self-destructive behavior. Remember Paddy Chayevsky's marvelous movie satire of television, *Network*[5] in which an anchor man (played by Peter Finch) announces that he will commit suicide on the air to improve his slipping ratings? That was a movie, but in real life (as we still call it) Chris Chubbuck, an anchor woman in Sarasota, Florida, worried about her ratings, announced on the air, one day in 1974, "In keeping with Channel 40's policy of bringing you the

---

4. For a brief synpopsis of the 1985 hijacking, see Laura King, *Mastermind of Achille Lauro Hijacking a Force in Palestinian Politics,* S.F. CHRON., May 19, 1998, at A12.

5. NETWORK (United Artists 1976).

latest in blood and guts in living color, you're going to see another first—an attempt at suicide." Whereupon she pulled a pistol out of a shopping bag and shot herself fatally in the head—on camera.

Chris Chubbuck could not benefit from the improvement in Channel 40's ratings. But this year Channel 7 in Miami, long at the bottom of the ratings pile and having lost its NBC network affiliation, emerged as one of the most successful independent stations in the nation. And, noted the *Wall Street Journal*, "a trend-setter for the entire television industry." How? Well, on the 6:30 news on one typical evening, Channel 7 reported on three rapes, two plane crashes, three hit and run accidents, a wild monkey attack, and the theft of false breasts—possibly by transvestites.

The quest of ratings by sensation and violence is not limited to the entertainment studio, but has spread to the once sacred precincts of the newsroom—in case you can still tell the difference. For the "docu-drama," and, more recently, the syndicated "reality-based" shows, as they are called, have almost erased the line between fact and fiction, between the actual and the re-created. And since the re-created has the advantage of being able to dramatize what the news cameras may not have seen, the news programmers are sometimes driven to re-creation themselves. As when, four years ago, the ABC Evening News showed a simulation, not immediately identified as such, of an American diplomat suspected of espionage handing over a briefcase full of secrets to a Russian agent.

That's show biz for you! I shall never forget broadcasting live from Holland on CBS, reporting man-in-the-street reaction to the moon landing. One Dutch citizen said he was not impressed—he liked it better the first time, when it was clearer. It finally dawned on me, as I "tossed" back to anchorman Walter Cronkite, in New York, that my Hollander had seen a simulation of the moon landing an hour earlier and didn't know the difference.

And I suspect that kids who go around shooting kids, on purpose, or at random, no longer know the difference between the bang-bang they grow up with on the television screen and the bang-bang that snuffs out real lives. Maybe the kids they shoot will come back to life after the commercial. The de-sensitizing effect of endless repetition of violent acts is the most destructive aspect of television's general assault on a sense of reality.

I am old enough to remember an America, and a world, without television. Indeed, I can remember seeing this new toy demonstrated by RCA at the New York World's Fair in 1939. In pre-television days, you could see blood and thunder in the movies, but coming out of the theater, you came back to reality. In those days, when President Roosevelt delivered his radio fireside chats, there was no temptation to go channel-hopping because there were no channels to hop to. In those days, writer E. B. White predicted that television would become "the test of the modern world, "a saving radiance," or "a new and unbearable disturbance of the modern peace."[6]

That was more than a half century ago. Would you care to vote in an opinion poll: saving radiance or unbearable disturbance?

Violence (and sex) on television have not developed by happenstance. In the 1950s, ABC, the youngest and least watched of the three networks, found a formula to catch up with NBC and CBS. It was *The Untouchables*, a program full of violence, sensationally successful, that established murder and mayhem as the way to lift ratings. Today's blood and guts in living color has come a long way since the fuzzy black and white mayhem of the sixties.

But, for all those years, violence has been embedded in the tissue of television. Scriptwriters will tell you that they are ordered to insert more scenes of sex and violence in their scenarios, and that scripts have been rejected for being too tame. And for all those years the networks, like the tobacco companies, have refused to acknowledge that their product presents a national health risk.

"The most important thing," said the Surgeon General, "is that a causal relationship has been shown between violence viewing and aggression." Not the current Surgeon General, but Surgeon General Jesse Steinfeld in 1972. There had been studies before, and there have been studies since, to make that point. The most recent comes from the Commission on Violence and Youth of the American Psychological Association. It reported the level of violence on commercial television constant during two decades. In prime time, five to six violent acts per hour . . . twenty to twenty-five on Saturday morning children's programs. On cable television, like MTV, much more.[7] The Report says:

> There is absolutely no doubt that higher levels of viewing on television are correlated with increased acceptance of aggressive attitudes and increased aggressive behavior. . . . Children's exposure to violence in the mass media, particularly at young ages, can have

---

6.   E.B. White, *One Man's Meat*, HARPER'S, Oct. 1938.

7.   AMERICAN PSYCHOLOGICAL ASSOCIATION, REPORT OF THE COMMISSION ON VIOLENCE AND YOUTH (1993).

harmful lifelong consequences.... Viewing violence increases
desensitization to violence, resulting in calloused attitudes towards
violence directed at others and a decreased likelihood to take action
on behalf of the victim of violence.[8]

But you have known all that for a long time, or at least to the
extent that the media would let you know it. Let me share with you a
little inside story. In 1968 CBS assigned me to cover the hearings of
the National Commission on the Causes and Prevention of Violence
named by President Johnson after the assassinations of Martin Luther
King and Robert Kennedy. One of its interim reports dealt with
television and violence, obviously a sensitive subject for television. I
taped a summary for the *Evening News*. Shortly before air time I was
told that CBS executives had intervened to censor my report. Deleted
from the tape was, among other things, a paragraph citing the view of
the Commission that while "most persons will not kill after seeing a
single violent television program . . . it is possible that many learn
some of their attitudes about violence from years of TV exposure and
may be likely to engage in violence." My protest against that self-
serving censorship was one of the times I almost got fired.

But television can no longer cover up its love affair with the
violence on the tube that helps to produce violence in the street.
Professor Brandon Centerwall of the University of Washington
calculates that if, hypothetically, television had never been invented,
violent crime in America would be about half what it is . . . 10,000
fewer homicides a year, 70,000 fewer rapes, 700,000 fewer injurious
assaults.

But television has been invented and, like nuclear energy, needs
to be tamed for peaceful purposes. The major networks, feeling the
heat, and fearing government intervention, now offer warning labels,
"Due to some violent content, parental discretion advised." For the
quarter of single-parent homes where the parent is usually at work,
who is there to exercise that discretion? And doesn't the label tend to
become a bait for kids that "here comes a good one"?

Congress has been looking at the problem of television and
violence since 1952, and now there is some sentiment in Congress to
control violence by legislation. One bill would mandate a chip enabling
viewers to block out programs that the networks classify as violent.
Networks are reluctant to put the label on for the obvious reason that
advertisers will stay away from such programs. Representative John

---

8. *Id.*

Bryant of Texas has a bill that says: cut violence or you will be fined and stations may lose license when they come up for renewal. In a Senate hearing, Howard Metzenbaum told network executives, "Do something or else." Of course, the "or else" raises First Amendment issues and, while the courts have held that a regulated industry, using channels that really belong to the public, cannot escape regulation, any move to regulate for content stirs profound unease in a supporter of free speech and free press. Nothing is more likely to bring on a threat to the First Amendment than abuse of the First Amendment. By law, after all, television is supposed to operate "in the public interest, convenience, and necessity."

But, why is it so hard to get television to control its love affair with violence? Because of perverse economic incentives. Because violence sells. And why does it sell? Because the public buys it. You are those rating points that make violence profitable.

I like the approach of Attorney General Janet Reno, who recommends that parents refuse to buy products that advertise on violent television programs. Does that sound like "boycott?" Yes, it does. But the problem of violence on television will not be resolved until the economic incentives are reversed. Better organized public action than government regulation.

Well, I have probably blown my chances for my next television contract, but nearing seventy-seven, I don't think I'm much of a threat to Rather, Jennings, and Brokaw anyway. Not that I ever was. But, at my age I am less concerned about what I do in television than in what television does to us. It was Edward R. Murrow (who, by the way, said that "if I were in charge of CBS, I am sure it would go broke") who warned against television becoming "insulation from the realities of the world." Were he alive today to witness some of the mind-scrambling effects of television on the human psyche, the conditioning for passivity and/or violence, I am sure he would consider his gloomiest forebodings more than realized. And E. B. White, who saw the coming age of television as a race "between the things that are and the things that seem to be," would doubtless shake his head at the victory of "seem to be."[9]

And remember White's words about "saving radiance" or "unbearable disturbance?"[10] We've had the disturbance for more than half a century. We wait for "the saving radiance."

---

9.   White, *supra* note 6.
10.   *Id.*

Theodore H. White Memorial Lecture[†]

This is a great honor for me—perhaps the greatest since appearing on the Nixon "enemies list." When Marvin[1] called to invite me to deliver the Theodore White Memorial Lecture, my first impulse was to say, "I thought you'd never ask."

This occasion has many warm associations for me. First of all, Teddy White, leader of my generation of journalists, who set the standard for the rest of us. Then, Joan Shorenstein Barone, who performed the improbable feat of being gentle and gracious while being a television producer. And Walter Shorenstein, who manages to be loved even though he gives money. He has been my friend since he volunteered, twenty-odd years ago, to drive me to the San Francisco airport after a lecture. And Marvin, whose life, family and interests have intertwined with mine since he first explained to me, in Moscow in 1956, what was between the lines of *Pravda*. And, the association with Harvard, which has sponsored some of the work of my wife, Li, and has seen to the education of my daughter, Lisa.

So, this is something of a family affair. But, wait, there's more. It is also a matter of pride, not to say awe, to be following to this podium Walter Cronkite and Ben Bradlee. (Senator Warren Rudman, not being a journalist, doesn't count.) Ah, those years at CBS when one tested a microphone by saying, "Well, Walter . . . well, Walter . . . well, Walter. . . ." And those years in Washington, with Ben Bradlee, as fearless and no-nonsense a journalist as I have ever known, even before he became Jason Robards.

Re-reading Walter's and Ben's lectures in preparation for mine, I am struck by the common theme of the elders of our craft re-examining where we are in the new media world. We have become uncomfortably aware that Americans don't love us so much any more and are no longer willing to forgive us our press passes. It's a long way from Hildy Johnson of *The Front Page* to the million-dollar blow-dried anchor person on television. Indeed, our whole profession seems

†. This speech was first presented at the John F. Kennedy School of Government, Joan Shorenstein Barone Center on the Press, Politics and Public Policy, Harvard University, Nov. 18, 1993.
    1. Marvin Kalb, Director of the Barone Center.

sometimes to have been crowded into a small corner of a vast entertainment stage—competing with entertainment and sometimes borrowing the tools and values of entertainment in a relentless quest for ratings. Reality yields to "reality-based," which is reality debased.

For the pain of self-doubt a little self-flagellation always provides relief. Dan Rather made a Murrowesque speech to the news directors in Miami, saying, "They've got us putting more fuzz and wuzz on the air . . . competing not with other news programs, but with entertainment programs . . . We should be ashamed of what we have done and not done, measured against what we could do." I don't know what Dan means precisely by "fuzz and wuzz," and whether he considers being teamed with Connie Chung an abdication to entertainment values. But, where do you draw the line? Surely, Dan must be aware of how entertainment value has contributed to his own success.

In the chorus of self-criticism, Peter Jennings tells *TV Guide* he wants to "pay more attention to what conservatives are saying." And Janet Malcolm of the *New Yorker* says that "every journalist who is not too stupid or too full of himself to notice what is going on knows that what he does is morally indefensible."[2] She sees the journalist as a kind of confidence man, preying on the people he deals with.

While I have some problems with the gospel according to Janet Malcolm, who has some ethics problems of her own, the question she raises is very much on people's minds. What is the interface between journalists and the people we interview, write about, put on the air? Are we courageous scourges of the "establishment," or have we grown into an establishment ourselves—more invasive, more overweening, more insensitive and more self-serving than the government and the political process we profess to monitor? And, is one establishment in bed with the other? In a word, who uses whom?

I shall never forget the cab driver, taking me from La Guardia airport to the Waldorf Astoria in 1974 to receive, with other CBS correspondents, an Emmy award for covering Watergate. "Mr. Schorr," he said, flattering me by recognizing me, "why don't you reporters tell us what's *really* going on in Washington?" When I remonstrated that I was about to get a prize for telling him what was going on, he shook his head. "You're all together, and you work out

---

2. *See* Linda Fibich, *Under Siege,* AM. JOURN. REV., Sept. 1995, at 16 (quoting Janet Malcolm from a 1989 article in the *New Yorker*).

between you when somebody is going to be dumped. But you're afraid to tell us what's *really* going on."

So, here was I, the quintessential outsider, accused of being an insider! But, how does it really work between the news media and the politicians? Who gains, who loses? Who uses whom, and is the public served by the process?

The question has to be examined at several levels because the interaction between press and politician has been changing over the years. The politicians have been gaining on us in sophisticated techniques for manipulation. But now, advancing technology of instantaneous worldwide communication makes life unpredictable for both of us.

Who uses whom? The traditional relationship is symbiotic, though we are reluctant to dwell on how often our successes are really someone else's successes.

For example, as CBS correspondent in Moscow in 1957, I received considerable credit for arranging the first-ever television interview with a Soviet leader—Nikita Khrushchev—from the Kremlin. (Not *live* from the Kremlin—those were the dark ages before satellites, before video tape, before color.) Now it can be told—the secret of that scoop. A Soviet official called me, referred to the latest of our monthly letters proposing an interview with Premier Nikolai Bulganin. The official asked if we were still interested in an interview with Nikita Khrushchev, head of the Communist Party. "Sure," I said, not mentioning that it was Bulganin we had asked for. So, the result was an hour of Nikita Khrushchev on American TV. President Eisenhower criticized CBS for letting the communist boss into America's living rooms. Why did it happen? Seen in retrospect, Khrushchev wanted to renew his relations with the West that had been torpedoed by the 1956 Soviet bloodbath in Hungary. He wanted American television to help him open a campaign that led, two years later, to a tour of America and a parley at Camp David. Our scoop; his coup. Another example: In 1963, working on a documentary on communist espionage in West Germany, I got an offer from the CIA—an interview with an East German intelligence officer who had just defected. He had stories to tell about how easy it was to penetrate West German security. The CIA wanted to needle the German government into a crackdown on spying. The interview in a Frankfurt safe house with Lieutenant Guenter Maennel helped my docu-mentary. I'm sure it helped the CIA.

Or, closer to home: In 1976 I obtained the draft of the final report of the House Intelligence Committee, recounting the failures and misdeeds of the CIA. The Ford Administration was trying, and eventually succeeded, in having the report suppressed by the House. I don't talk about sources, then or now. But let me say I'm fully aware I served somebody's purpose in a grim game of saving that report from the memory hole. Not to say that I didn't work hard to get it. But that's what you call a mutually beneficial arrangement (if you leave out the trouble I got into as a consequence).

But, now we're onto that oldest established feature of Who Uses Whom called "leaks," which are about as old as secrets. Leak is an interesting verb, originally intransitive. Something leaked, that is, seeped, escaped, oozed out. But the press and government have made it transitive. Something *is* leaked. Somebody leaks. There are "leakers" and there are "leaking sessions." Michael Kelly in the *New York Times* says that former Secretary of State Jim Baker spent thiry-five hours a week leaking at a high level, while David Gergen handled the lower level.

One must divide leaks into two categories—authorized and unauthorized. President Nixon and secretary Kissinger loved the one, hated the other. The Watergate White House files are full of references to 'this should be leaked to this columnist, that should be leaked to that magazine.' The Howard Hunt forgery of a cable linking President Kennedy to the assassination of Ngo Dien Diem was planned to be leaked to *Life* magazine. The information about a financial deal that drove Justice Abe Fortas from the Supreme Court was leaked to *Life* magazine.

But unplanned leaks, that is unplanned by them—drove Nixon and Kissinger up the wall and into wiretaps of officials and journalists, and into creating a leak-plugging unit called the Plumbers, which dealt, among other things, with the biggest unplanned leak of all—the Pentagon Papers.

Not everything that looks like a leak is a leak. Ben Bagdikian, writing about leaks in the *Columbia Journalism Review* in 1961, said that West German Chancellor Konrad Adenauer had "successfully leaked stories" to Flora Lewis, then of the *Washington Post*, and myself, then CBS correspondent in Bonn. The story in question, about Adenauer's criticism of President Kennedy at a closed-door session of his party caucus, had, in fact, not been deliberately leaked by anyone, but had been pieced together by strenuous efforts of four reporters working together. I wrote the *Colubia Journalism Review* to let Ben know that some stories are not given, but gotten.

There is also something that might be called the secondary leak. In January 1975, President Ford let slip, at a White House luncheon with the *New York Times* publisher, editors and columnists, that the CIA had been involved in assassination conspiracies. He then tried to retract by saying, "off the record." Publisher Arthur O. Sulzberger, to the distress of some of his staff, ordered that the explosive remark not be pursued. It came to my ears, resulting in an exclusive on the *CBS Evening News* that precipitated a Senate investigation and exposure of the CIA efforts, in league with the Mafia, to eliminate Fidel Castro.

Without discussing my Source, I can say that no one in authority in the U.S. Government or the *New York Times* wanted that leak, and neither benefited from it. The public, I submit, did benefit mightily. It exposed to daylight one of the darkest chapters in the CIA's history— a secret the agency had scandalously kept from the Warren Commission.

Anybody here curious about the identity of the most talked-about and speculated about leaker of modern times—Deep Throat? Have you wondered why somebody apparently so inside as to know what was going on would be so disloyal and take such chances? I believe that Jim Mann, who was a colleague of Bob Woodward's at the *Washington Post* and now works for the *Los Angles Times*, had it right in a very detailed and very convincing article in the *Atlantic Monthly*. "Deep Throat" was one or more of three top-level FBI officials, furious because Nixon had picked outsider L. Patrick Gray to succeed J. Edgar Hoover, furious also that Gray and the White House were obstructing their investigation of Watergate, which would make the bureau end up looking bad.

So, was the Watergate conspiracy punctured by G-men, jealous of their turf, jealous of the bureau's reputation? So, Woodward and Bernstein got the Pulitzer prize, and the FBI got Nixon. Who used whom?

And, speaking of Nixon, would it amuse you to learn that recently I was the beneficiary of a leak from old "enemies list" Nixon himself? He had written a memorandum about how President Bush was missing the boat on aid to Russia, and circulated it to a list of friends that did not include me. My friend Bill Safire showed it to me, but stipulated that I couldn't use it without Nixon's permission. I noticed that the memo lacked any secret or confidential label or any of the security cautions that came so naturally to Nixon. So, I called Nixon's office in New Jersey and asked his assistant to ask him whether I could quote from it. She said it would not be necessary to consult him—she knew it would be all right. Sounded as though she had been waiting for my call. So, I got a story, and Nixon, as he undoubtedly planned, put a shot across President Bush's bow in a way that enabled him to say it wasn't a press release, just a private memorandum that leaked. Leaked? Was leaked?

In the current phase of our public life, the leak has become so commonplace as to be devalued. Television correspondents can routinely report what the President is going to say in a speech tomorrow. Names of prospective nominees are floated and often withdrawn without regard to their reputations. There is hardly an official report, starting with the budget, that you will not find summarized before it is released. Whatever happened to the embargo—that mutually convenient arrangement between press and government?

The leak has now been absorbed into the all-embracing Spin. Secret-keeping has fallen to image-making. Massaging the media, the care and feeding of the media, have come almost to overshadow policy-making and decision-making. First we have the feeding of the press, then the feedback. If that is negative, you then see changes called "fine-tuning." The Clinton health program, in nine months of gestation and trial balloons, went through so much fine-tuning as to be worthy of an orchestra. The White House image-making corps grows steadily larger. David Gergen, the communicator, is now also the policy advisor. The danger is the communicating will become not only a way of explaining policy, but will dictate and ultimately become the policy.

Spin patrol, damage control, message of the day . . . the process has become so ingrained as to make governing seem like a form of theater. No one was better at it than President Reagan. At CNN, one of my functions was to attend Reagan news conferences and then do instant analysis from the White House lawn. Typically, I would start by saying, "Mr. Reagan made these five factual errors tonight." That would only bring calls and letters of protest about bias against the president. Who uses whom? Surely I did nothing to Reagan.

President Clinton has added another dimension to governing by theater. He has effectively hijacked television from the journalists by talking over their heads to town meetings, MTV and Larry King. Reporters, columnists and commentators have become supplicants, waiting to be invited to one of the more intimate luncheons with the President so they can write something he has not already said live. (I have yet to be invited to any such thing. But, never mind, I can always have lunch with Nixon.)

It is curious that President Clinton, who has commanded more media exposure than any president in history, complains that he is not getting across the story of his accomplishments. On NBC's *Meet the Press* the other day, he quoted people in his home town as saying, "There must be a conspiracy to keep this a secret." And he ruminated about whether "this may be my fault, or it may be somebody else's." Who uses whom? The President cannot complain of a lack of access to the public. If he comes off, in the end, as less than coherent, he will have to consult his scattershot style, his handlers or his policies.

And now we come to the next stage of Who Uses Whom—the stage in which television takes control out of the hands of press and policy-maker alike. President Reagan saw on television relatives of hostages in Lebanon blaming him for not doing enough to bring home their loved ones. Reagan saw in the pictures a political problem and he launched his ransom-by-arms-sales initiative.

President Bush, having decided to get American troops quickly home from the Gulf War in 1991, suddenly became aware that America was looking at frightful scenes of Kurds in flight from Iraqi genocide, and he sent the troops back. He said, "No one can see the pictures . . . and not be deeply moved." When Americans are moved, a politician moves.

Television scenes of suffering in Bosnia led President Clinton to join in a humanitarian aid effort, and to promise more than he was able to deliver in protecting the Muslims. Somalia is a classic case of pictures dictating policy. In Somalia, scenes of starvation drew America into humanitarian, and then military, intervention. Later, scenes of an American prisoner and an American soldier's dead body being dragged through the streets drove the president to order withdrawal from Somalia.

National Security Adviser Anthony Lake confessed that "the pictures helped make us recognize that the military situation in Mogadishu had deteriorated in a way that we had not frankly recognized." Not a message from the Commander—the pictures!

Secretary of State Warren Christopher made a remarkable statement before the Senate Foreign Relations Committee two weeks ago: "Television is a wonderful phenomenon and sometimes even an instrument of freedom. But television images cannot be the North Star of America's foreign policy."

Can't they, though? Surely, the constant lurches in policy don't happen for no reason at all. Far ahead of the coming information highway, we have something close to an interactive system of formulating policy, and the instantaneity of modern television makes it necessary to formulate policy on the run.

How it was in the old days is recalled by Richard Reeves in his fine book, *President Kennedy*.[3] He reports how I covered, for CBS, the beginning of the Berlin Wall early Sunday morning, August 13, 1961. By the time the film reached New York and got on the air on the next available news program, the Kennedy staff had time to read their cables, consult their allies and decide how to react. If that had happened today, officials would see the event along with all Americans, and would have to scramble for a public response.

In any event, the picture is far from the whole reality. But images tend to replace reality, or to create their own reality. We are spellbound by pictures of the assault on the parliament in Moscow and on the Ostenkino television center (which may have been the more crucial battleground) but we are given little understanding of what is happening behind the facade. We know what television does, but where is journalism? Catching up more slowly, less vividly on radio and in print, with less impact on policy, less impact on the people who make what passes for policy in the television age.

That, to a lesser extent, is true also in domestic policy. When policy is driven by television, it is driven by the reality that television creates. Vivid displays of violence, including juvenile violence, create an impression of rates of violent crime out of control. In fact, FBI statistics indicate violent crime decreasing in large cities in recent years. But, there are higher ratings to be found in blood and gore than in statistics. So the reality on which government proceeds is slightly altered. So great is the obsession with perception and spin that the spin tends to become the policy. If projections of forty percent of Americans paying more for health care create a firestorm, no problem. Tomorrow we will have new projections.

If the news media play up stories like the President's haircut, the White House travel office and the suicide of Vincent Foster, it may be, in part, because these are among the few remaining "spontaneous" stories—stories that have eluded the handlers and the spin doctors.

---

3. RICHARD REEVES, PRESIDENT KENNEDY: PROFILE OF POWER (1993).

Who uses whom? We journalists have tried so hard to serve as guardians of reality, only to be no longer sure if there is a reality and if our own bosses care about it. The spin doctors are gaining on us, but technology is gaining on all of us. In the Gulf War, the censors did a pretty good job of controlling coverage. In the landing on the Somalia beach, television made a mockery of the best laid plans of mice and managers. In the next war involving Americans, news management may be defeated by the latest wrinkles in minicams, portable dishes and cellular phones.

For sixty years I have loved journalism, not always wisely, but well. I have loved the news profession, not always the news industry. Teddy White would have understood about that. Some forty-five years ago E.B. White saw the coming age of television as a race "between things that are and the things that seem to be."[4] I think he would say today that "seem to be" seems to be far ahead. I hope a younger generation of journalists will run hard to reclaim "the things that are."

---

4.   E.B. White, *One Man's Meat,* HARPER'S, Oct. 1938.

The Nixon Legacy†

Nixon is back! As a subject of American fascination, that is.

The twentieth anniversary of his resignation on August 8th, the revealing diaries of his former chief of staff, H. R. Haldeman, the reexaminations of Watergate in print (by British correspondent, Fred Emery) and on television (I narrated a five-part mini-series for the Discovery Channel on cable TV) have combined to reawaken interest among those who had almost forgotten and stir interest among those too young to have known.

And the end is not yet in sight in research into the driven President who was the first ever to be driven from office. The basic story of Nixon's plunge to destruction is known—the man so angry at his opponents, so fearful of his "enemies" that he was propelled into extra-legal response—wiretaps, surveillance, break-ins—and then into a criminal obstruction of justice to hide what he had done.

But there are still caves to explore for new Dead Sea Scrolls in the forty-two million pages of documents and the 4,000 hours of Nixon tape in the hands of the National Archives. (All the tapes released in the investigation of Watergate amount to only sixty hours.) Nixon lawyers are still resisting the release of the remaining tapes, a source of great frustration to the archivists who have spent years preparing them for release.

There are no earth-shaking revelations to be expected from this material, but they will give us a deeper understanding of the Nixon phenomenon. For example, one early tape shows Nixon's tendency to invent a persona for himself—even with his closest advisers. Meeting alone with Soviet Ambassador Anatoli Dobrynin, the President, in measured tones, asks whether the Soviet Government can intercede with North Vietnam to come to the peace table. A little while later, Nixon reports on the conversation to Haldeman, representing himself as having been much sterner with Dobrynin than he actually was. Shortly thereafter, he briefs National Security Adviser Henry Kissinger by now making himself appear to have been quite tough with the ambassador. He quotes himself as saying, "See here, Anatoli!"

---

†. This speech was originally presented at the Paepcke Auditorium, Aspen Institute for Humanistic Studies, Aspen, Colorado, Aug. 19, 1994.

which are words he never spoke to Dobrynin nor, in fact, to anybody on the 950 reels of tape.

It is interesting also to compare the diary that Nixon kept on dictabelt apart from his tapes, with the diary of H. R. Haldeman. For example, on August 3, 1972—six weeks after the Watergate break-in—Nixon's diary entry has him, in conversation with Haldeman and John Erlichman, saying that he has been "above reproach" in not using the power of government to go after his enemies. Haldeman's version of the same conversation has Nixon talking about the need to "get some action" from the IRS and Justice Department against "people supporting the opposition."

Treasury Department aide Joshua Steiner could have taken lessons from Nixon in how to smooth out your own diary. But I can personally vouch for the accuracy of Haldeman's version, having been the subject of an FBI investigation and an IRS audit ordered by Nixon. Indeed, "abuse of power"—the use of government to harass his "enemies"—became Article II of the three Articles of Impeachment voted by the House Judiciary Committee in the Summer of 1974.[1]

As recent disclosures—especially the Haldeman diaries—bring us closer to the inner Nixon, he gets worse and worse. He discussed with Dr. Kissinger the need to keep the Vietnam War going and achieve a settlement timed to precede the 1972 election. He was against racial integration and did not like black people. He wanted to replace black waiters in the White House. He identified Jews with the lobby for legalizing marijuana and talked of Jewish "domination" of the arts and the media. He hated the press and the intellectual "elite," denigrating the value of a college education. He disliked the civil service ("ninety-six percent of the bureaucracy are against us—they're bastards who are out to screw us.").

Yet, somehow he managed to keep that seething volcano of hatreds and fears under enough control to win two elections—the second with an unprecedented majority. One searches still for understanding of the Nixon who could lead Americans while harboring hatred against so many of them. Nixonology becomes an exercise as much in pathology as in political science.

Combing the latest revelations for a better understanding of why it all happened, I arrive at a new realization of how prone Nixon was to act on false premises bordering on self-delusion. He not only said things that were untrue, but apparently believed things that were

---

1. H.R. REP. NO. 93-1305, at 1-4 (1974).

untrue, and the line between deception and self-deception was often blurred. Here are four examples:

The Bay of Pigs "Secrets"

President Nixon spoke often to aides about some deeply concealed scandal—an assassination, or something on that order—connected with the Bay of Pigs invasion of Cuba in 1961 and involving President Kennedy and the CIA. He saw it as something that could be used as ammunition against his political opponents.

His aide, Charles Colson, has said that "nailing" Kennedy on the Bay of Pigs was a "pet Nixon project." Meeting with Haldeman, John Ehrlichman, and John Mitchell on September 18, 1971, Nixon said he wanted the "full secret file" on the Bay of Pigs delivered to him by the CIA, "or else!"

Although there is no indication that he ever got the file he wanted, Nixon felt sure enough of his ground to use the Bay of Pigs as a form of pressure on the CIA to take responsibility for the Watergate break-in and, thereby, to halt the FBI's investigation. On June 23, 1973—in the fatal "smoking gun" tape—Nixon instructed Haldeman to remind CIA director Richard Helms that "we have protected him against a helluva lot of things" and that the FBI's Watergate investigation threatened to "blow the whole Bay of Pigs thing, which we think would be very unfortunate for the CIA and the country."

A mystified Haldeman went into Ehrlichman's office, saying, "Guess what? It's Bay of Pigs time again!" But, carrying out his assignment, Haldeman told Helms what he was instructed to say, only to have Helms explode, "The Bay of Pigs has nothing to do with this! I have no concern about the Bay of Pigs."

To this day, Helms vows that he had not the foggiest idea what dark secret about the Bay of Pigs Nixon believed he could use to get the CIA to stall the FBI investigation.

The Diem Assassination "Plot"

It is a matter of record that the Kennedy Administration supported the coup that resulted in the ouster and death of South Vietnamese President Ngo Dien Diem on November 1, 1963 (three weeks before Kennedy's assassination). But, Nixon spoke as though he believed that Kennedy was personally responsible for Diem's assassination, and he repeatedly issued orders to his aides to come up with the proof.

On June 17, 1971, Nixon ordered Kissinger to get him the "files on the murder of Diem." Next day he ordered Ehrlichman to have "the full Diem story" on his desk by the end of the week. When the information was not forthcoming, Nixon approved the assignment of one member of the secret new "Plumbers" investigative unit—E. Howard Hunt, a former CIA officer who described himself as "resident White House expert on the origins of the Vietnam War"—to track down the evidence of Kennedy's complicity. With another Plumber, G. Gordon Liddy, Hunt combed the Pentagon and State Department files, eventually reporting to Colson the suspicious circumstance, that the closer they got to the date of the coup, the thinner the files became.

Despite the lack of evidence, President Nixon went public, at his news conference on September 16, 1971, with the statement that "the way we got into Vietnam was through overthrowing Diem and the complicity in the murder of Diem."

The next step was to manufacture the proof. Using White House and State Department typewriters, copies of existing cables and a razor blade, Hunt forged messages in which the White House purportedly advised the American command in Saigon of decisions "at the highest level meeting" that Diem should be offered no assistance or asylum if he sought to escape the coup.

Life magazine, offered the cables for publication, found them suspicious. The forgeries were among the items in Hunt's White House safe removed after Watergate by presidential counsel John Dean and destroyed. Nixon knew (from Ehrlichman) about the forged cables, but seemed to regard them as simply replacing the real assassination proof his enemies had destroyed.

The "Bugged" Campaign Plane

It was an article of faith for Nixon that all the dirty tricks, surveillance and wiretaps he sponsored were simply getting back to Democrats who had done the same things. As a dramatic example, he often said that in 1968 the FBI had bugged his campaign plane on orders from President Johnson.

The FBI had, in fact, wiretapped the Watergate apartment of Anna Chennault, a Nixon supporter who was suspected by the Johnson White House of using her contacts in Saigon to forestall an "October surprise" peace settlement that would have helped the election chances of Vice President Hubert Humphrey. But, despite warnings from President Nixon that he would fire anybody withholding the facts from him, the FBI insisted that there had been no eavesdropping on Nixon's campaign plane.

Nonetheless, Nixon felt sure enough of his supposition to use it as a weapon to try to forestall a Senate Watergate investigation. On January 9, 1973, Nixon discussed "the Johnson bugging process" with Haldeman and said that if this could be "cranked up, LBJ could turn off the whole congressional investigation."

The threat to disclose "the Johnson bugging process" was relayed to the LBJ ranch, producing a counter-threat from the ex-president. According to Haldeman, Johnson responded by calling Cartha D. ("Deke") DeLoach, J. Edgar Hoover's top assistant and saying that "if the Nixon people are going to play with this, he would release. . . ."

The next words are, "deleted material—national security." This is the only deletion in the several hundred pages of Haldeman diaries made when the document was submitted for National Security Council review during the Carter Administration. DeLoach recently told me that the reference was to something classified at a level higher than top secret and still too sensitive to divulge.

Whatever it was, it apparently dissuaded Nixon from any further pressure on Johnson over the "bugged campaign plane."

The Hughes-O'Brien Threat

If one looks for the Nixon phobia that was most directly responsible for the Watergate break-in, it was the fear that Democratic National Chairman Lawrence O'Brien possessed some dreadful secret about Nixon's dealings with the eccentric industrialist, Howard Hughes, that would be sprung to damage Nixon at some crucial moment.

Since 1968, O'Brien had been on a retainer of some $200,000 a year from the Hughes organization. His contact was Robert Maheu, Executive Director of Hughes Enterprises. Maheu never saw the reclusive Hughes—they communicated entirely by memo. But Maheu handled all of Hughes' political activities for fifteen years. He presumably knew about a then-secret 1956 Hughes loan to Nixon's brother, Donald, and Donald's continuing relationship with the Hughes empire. More menacing, Maheu had handled an illegal "campaign" contribution of $100,000 from Hughes, given in cash after the 1968 campaign to the president's friend, Bebe Rebozo, and held in a safe deposit box in Key Biscayne, Florida, as a kind of secret nest egg for the president.

Nixon often talked to his aides about "going after" O'Brien because of his Hughes retainer, without mentioning his worry about his own Hughes "retainer." Typical of many Haldeman notations was one for March 4, 1970, that the president "wants us to move hard on Larry O'Brien." There were repeated admonitions to "follow up on the O'Brien-Hughes money," for Ehrlichman to "get off his tail on the O'Brien matter." The Internal Revenue Service was ordered to audit O'Brien's taxes and found nothing wrong.

In May 1972, as plans were made for the Gordon Liddy "political intelligence project," word sifted down from on high that O'Brien was to be a principal target. Colson told campaign aide Jeb Magruder to "get off the stick and get the Liddy project approved, so we can get information from O'Brien." Specifically, said Colson, "the information regarding the Florida dealings," an elliptical reference to the Rebozo cache of Hughes money.

Only slowly did it dawn on Liddy, as he wrote in his book, that the purpose of the two break-ins at Democratic National Committee headquarters in the Watergate—where the Plumbers set a wiretap and photographed documents—was "to find out what O'Brien had of a derogatory nature about us, not for us to get something on him."[2]

Three days after the June 17, 1972 break-in, it seemed also to dawn on President Nixon that he had sparked it. The tape of June 20 (the one with the notorious 18 1/2 minute gap) has him saying to Haldeman, "You know, I was on Colson's tail for six months to nail Larry O'Brien on the Hughes deal. Colson told me he was going to get the information one way or another. And that was O'Brien's office they were bugging, wasn't it?"

And, on March 13, 1973, Nixon tried to explain to John Dean, who said he was still mystified about the break-in when "anybody who's been around a national committee knows there's nothing there." The president started, "Well, the point is they were trying to see what the (unintelligible) developed in terms of the . . ." Nixon halted in mid-sentence, probably having second thoughts about confiding in Dean about his deepest fear.

And, irony of ironies, Nixon's desperation was for naught. O'Brien, who died in 1990, said he never knew about the Hughes

---

2. *See* G. GORDON LIDDY, THE MONKEY HANDLERS (1991).

money. "If I had known, you wouldn't have to break into my office to get it. I would have told the whole world."

All those demons and dragons—the Kennedys, their henchmen, the FBI and CIA, and who knows what else—haunted Nixon's dreams, beckoning him to misuse of power that would destroy his presidency.

Twenty years later, does it matter? Yes, it does. In the course of contending with his demons, Nixon revealed that a president can lie, cheat, break laws, strike at his foes with the weapons of government and subvert the meaning of constitutional government.

He shattered the assumption of regularity in the White House. He made Watergate the scale on which all future scandals involving the White House would be measured. It seemed natural when Senator Alfonse D'Amato (R-N.Y.), during the just-concluded Senate hearings on Whitewater, echoed the famous Howard Baker question on Watergate, "What did the president know and when did he know it?"

Americans once trusted presidents, even though history revealed that they had not always played straight with the public. President Johnson, by dissembling about the Vietnam War, established a contemporaneous presidential credibility gap. President Nixon widened it into a creditability chasm. Since Nixon, no president has been fully trusted. For a long time to come, none may be. That may be the final legacy of the driven man who almost drove constitutional government off the rails.

Imagining a Global Community†

Here, on a university campus, I am reminded that it is fifty-five years since I graduated from college in New York. One way of measuring time, and how our world has changed, is to recall some of the things commonplace today that we did not have.

We didn't have nylon or Saran wrap, or ball-point pens or atom bombs, or frozen foods or plastic credit cards, or jet planes or Xerox machines. In those days, chips were made of wood, hardware was hammers, and software wasn't in the dictionary. In those days grass was something you mowed, Coke was something you drank and pot was something you cooked in.

And we did not have television, a primal force perhaps as great as nuclear energy, and equally in need of taming for peaceful purposes, I can remember the first demonstration of television in America by RCA at the New York World's Fair 1939. I stood in from of a camera and my girlfriend could see me on a monitor a hundred feet away. It seemed like an interesting toy. I didn't see how it would ever amount to anything important.

And we did not have the United Nations. The League of Nations had withered on the vine, impotent to protect Ethiopia against Italian aggression by sanctions. Or to save Spain from being devastated by what was called a civil war, but was really a rehearsal ground for Hitler and Mussolini, preparing for a wider war.

So then came World War II and I, drafted into the army, was anxious to be sent to Europe, where I had always wanted to be a correspondent. And so the responsive military sent me to San Antonio to serve in what we called the army occupation in Texas. At HQ 4th Army, Fort Sam Houston, peacocks roamed the quadrangle because the commanding general liked peacocks. There I was when President Roosevelt died, and when V-E Day came, and when the B-29 Enola Gay dropped the first atom bomb on Hiroshima, and when the Japanese surrendered, as many think they had been on the point of doing anyway.

Amid the ruins of World War II the victorious leaders imagined again a global community. The wartime coalition had been named the

---

†. This speech was originally presented as Remarks by Daniel Schorr, Mansfield Conference, University of Montana, Missoula, Oct. 24, 1994.

United Nations, so now the United Nations would be made permanent. It would rest on a consensus of two great powers, the United States and the Soviet Union; two no longer so great, Great Britain and France; and one hoping to become great, China. And these five together, each with a veto to protect its position, would lead colonial possessions into a brave new world of independence, and together the five would police the world and keep it peaceful.

They really imagined a global community. But they had erected their structure on a San Andreas faultline of ideological antagonism between communism and capitalism, between East and West. The fault line had been subordinated to the common purpose of defeating Germany and Japan, but once that had been accomplished, the fault line began to rumble again.

Within two years, Stalin had bared his teeth in Eastern Europe and Winston Churchill was proclaiming something called the Iron Curtain. An ideological contest started, called the Cold War. The West launched massive rearmament and organized itself into a North Atlantic alliance. NATO's purpose, said Lord Ismay, its first executive secretary, was "to keep the Russians out, the Americans in and the Germans down."

In our arrogance, we divided the globe into three parts, the First World—us of course. The Second World, where Stalin reigned. And then all the rest, something loosely—very loosely—called the Third World. Third World, if a somewhat ethnocentric term, was meant benevolently. It was the undeveloped world—later, with a fine sense of nuance, changed to *under*developed world. *It* was the part of the world that the advanced guardians, acting together, would lead into independence, into nation building, into economy building.

Instead, the Third World became an area of struggle between First and Second World superpowers. They chose and armed states, and factions within states, for a series of proxy wars. An open war in Korea and Vietnam. Less formal wars in Ethiopia, Somalia, Angola, Cambodia and Chile, Guatemala and Nicaragua. Even in South Africa, the communist-supported African National Congress did not receive our seal of approval until the Cold War was over.

The Cold War was my beat. From 1948 I covered the Marshall Plan, which President Truman sold to Congress as a way of resisting the communists, and the birth of NATO. I was serving in Moscow in 1956, when Nikita Khrushchev sent tanks to crush the anti-communist uprising in Hungary, and the Eisenhower Administration, fearing to unleash nuclear war, stood on the sidelines. In 1957 the first two orbiting Sputniks were launched, one with a dog aboard, and the arms race developed into a race for predominance in space.

In Germany, in 1961, I witnessed the visual symbol of how World War III might start. The Wall had gone up in Berlin in August, and in October a dispute developed over the right of American officials to cross freely into East Berlin. (Remember, Berlin was technically under four-power occupation.) Soon American and Soviet tanks were facing each other almost muzzle to muzzle at Checkpoint Charlie. I stood between them and wondered whether this is how the world ends. But, as I later learned, this was a photo opportunity for political purposes. In private President Kennedy and Khrushchev were busy backing off from the confrontation.

So, in 1989, the Berlin Wall came down, and the Second World collapsed and, hooray, our First World team had won. And we were ready to survey the fruits and the costs of the Cold War which, for both sides, had provided such an automatic and unthinking organizing principle.

We learned of some of the unspeakable things that, in the course of holy crusade against the other, we had done to our own countries and peoples. In the former Soviet Union, vast ecological disasters. The Aral Sea, the world's largest inland sea, drying up, becoming a scene of environmental and economic disaster. Thousands of people blithely exposed to radiation in the course of nuclear weapons development that almost ignored safeguards. Was America, leader of the First World, much better? In time, we learned of the nonchalance of the managers of our nuclear facilities about radiation effects on the areas around them. And, worse, hundreds—perhaps thousands—of Americans turned into guinea pigs for experiments with plutonium. In forty years of Cold War, the casualties were almost entirely limited to what each superpower did to its own people and its own environment—and to the Third World.

As after World War I, as after World War II, so after the Cold War once again the idea arose of a global community. Mikhail Gorbachev gave it its name—New World Order—and President Bush embraced it. The New World Order was based on the premise of an American-Soviet partnership that would keep a checkrein on regional animosities and promote the general welfare. But Gorbachev's Soviet Union collapsed, leaving us not with a partner, but with a dependent.

And what of the Third World that we were going to nurture and bring into the dawn of a new day? There we had left warring clans with weapons, a legacy of the Cold War, weapons that they could now use to kill each other. We have not done much to change the lethal mix of too many people, driven to prey on their environment and on each other. Why genocide in Rwanda? Rwanda, where the average woman has 8.5 children, has the highest population density in Africa. Why will Haiti have so much trouble making it? Haiti's population is seven million, expected to double in eighteen years. And Haiti is almost entirely deforested.

And what is the First World doing for the Third World? One-fifth of the world's population uses two-thirds of the world's resources and gives back four-fifths of the world's waste and pollutants.

Before we can imagine again a global community there are some words out of our Cold War lexicon that need to be re-defined. One is *aggression*, which is not just a matter of marching across a border with an army. Aggression can be committed by despoiling an environment, by denying people a chance of future livelihood. Another word is *security*, which is not just safety against bombs and guns, but against the less obvious threats created by pollution and by population, including people on the move. President Clinton was using a new definition of security when he said that one reason for sending troops to Haiti was to preserve "the security of our borders." Was Cedras going to invade? No, this meant security against a desperate exodus of Haitians. And another word that needs a broader definition is *violence*. A child that dies of plague or AIDS dies violently. When an arid region is deprived of unpolluted water, violence has been committed. We must (pardon the paraphrase) take arms against a troubled sea.

So, now, if we are to imagine a global community, we must imagine a community that can organize against new kinds of aggression, and new kinds of violence into a new kind of collective security.

My friend, Tim Wirth, Undersecretary of State, uses the phrase "human security." "Human security" is about the billion people who live in abject poverty, the 800 million people who go hungry every day, the 17 million who die each year from preventable diseases. And the 1.3 billion without access to clean water, the 2 billion who lack safe sanitation. Not to mention the 20 million who move across borders, escaping from destitution or from each other.

So, we are ready to try to imagine again a global community to deal with these disasters. I wish I could simply say "United Nations." But the United Nations is not much more than the authority and the resources that are invested in it. And recent administrations—the Bush and the Clinton Administrations—have had some unsatisfactory experiences with the U.N. in Bosnia and in Somalia. The United States has shown a tendency to pull back from the whole concept of universal multilateralism.

So perhaps we need something less universal that America would be ready to support and lead and entrust with some of our precious sovereignty.

Perhaps we should look to an institution regarded as a great success, one that America has always been happy about and comfortable with. I am speaking of NATO, a collective security alliance that needs only a new definition of "security" to give it a new mission of deterring "violence" and "aggression." And organizing for Human Security.

I don't care much whether NATO recasts itself or whether some new kind of alliance is created. I care only that an institution be created in which America can function effectively, dedicated to the cause of human security in a world no longer divided into First, Second and Third Worlds, but just *One World*.

Ten Days That Shook the White House[†]

Score one for the power of the media, especially television, as a policy-making force. Coverage of the massacre and exodus of the Kurds generated public pressures that were instrumental in slowing the hasty American military withdrawal from Iraq and forcing a return to help guard and care for the victims of Saddam Hussein's vengeance.

The Kurdish tragedy was only one in a season of worldwide disasters—the typhoon in Bangladesh, earthquakes in Soviet Georgia and Costa Rica, famine in Africa. Scenes of suffering flitted past American television audiences, a succession of miseries almost too rapid and stark to be absorbed.

But the suffering of the Kurds stood out from the others. This was not a natural catastrophe, but a man-made disaster, and one that had a special claim on the American conscience. It was America, after all, that had invaded Iraq and shaken loose the underpinnings of authority. It was America's president, George Bush, who, on February 15, called on the "Iraqi military and the Iraqi people" to rise up and "force Saddam Hussein . . . to step aside." It was President Bush who, on February 27, had ordered an abrupt cessation of hostilities, leaving the Iraqi dictator with enough armor and aircraft to put down Shiite and Kurdish uprisings. And, finally, it was the Bush Administration that, after first warning the Iraqi regime not to use helicopter gunships against its own people, then stood by while they were used to strafe Kurds fleeing to the mountains in the north.

Americans became dimly aware, in the month after the war stopped and the rebellions had started, that their government, having burst the floodgates in Iraq, was trying to run away from the flood. There was even a whisper of tacit collusion with the dictator whom Bush had called "worse than Hitler." The *New York Times* reported on March 27 that the Administration had "decided to let President Saddam Hussein put down rebellions in his country without American intervention."[1] This in the name of avoiding being dragged into what the president called "a Vietnam-style quagmire," and in response to

---

  †. This article was originally published under the same title at COLUM. JOURN. REV. 21 (July/Aug. 1991). Reprinted with permission.
  1. Andrew Rosenthal, *After The War*, N.Y. TIMES, Mar. 27, 1991, at A1.

Saudi Arabian and Turkish concerns about the possible disintegration of Iraq.[2]

The Administration had every reason, at first, to believe that the public supported a policy of getting the troops home quickly and avoiding involvement in ethnic strife. There was some criticism, but it was mainly confined to the editorial pages of newspapers. The Bush Administration, like the Reagan Administration, seems to work on the premise that print does not move people: only television, with its visceral impact, does.

The Kurds had been let down by America before. As disclosed in the report of the House Intelligence Committee in 1976 (of which I obtained a draft before the House voted to suppress it), President Nixon had the CIA sponsor a Kurdish uprising against Saddam Hussein, starting in 1972, as a favor to the Shah of Iran. When the Shah and Saddam settled their differences, support for the insurrection was withdrawn and the Kurds were abandoned to an Iraqi attack. ("Our movement and people are being destroyed in an unbelievable way, with silence from everyone," Mustafa Barzani, father of the current Kurdish leader, wrote to Secretary of State Henry Kissinger on March 10, 1975. "We feel, Your Excellency, that the United States has a moral and political responsibility towards our people, who have committed themselves to your country's policy."). Thousands were killed and 200,000 fled to Iran, of whom 40,000 were forcibly returned to Iraq.

I reported this on CBS in 1976, but it was a "tell story" without the pictures needed to let the audience experience the dimensions of American betrayal. And it made little impression. So now, in March 1991, the Bush Administration was not overly concerned with "tell stories" and commentaries about how America was turning its back on the Kurds.

Jim Hoagland wrote in the *Washington Post* of "an American bug-out from the Persian Gulf,"[3] and William Safire wrote in the *New York Times* that the president had experienced "a failure of nerve."[4] But "a senior presidential aide" told *Time* magazine, "The only pressure for the U.S. to intervene is coming from columnists and

---

2. *Id.*

3. Jim Hoagland, *Don't Bug Out—This Isn't Vietnam,* WASH. POST, May 2, 1991, at A19.

4. William Safire, *Bush's Bay of Pigs,* N.Y. TIMES, Apr. 4, 1991, at A23.

commentators."[5] And a "top White House aide" (probably Chief of Staff John Sununu in both cases) told *Newsweek*, "a hundred Safire columns will not change the public's mind. There is no political downside to our policy."[6]

Famous last words, politically speaking. What the White House did not seem to realize was that, by the end of March, the issue, as perceived by the public, was changing from military intervention in support of a revolution to compassionate intercession for the victims of Saddam Hussein's genocidal methods. By then, while hundreds of thousands of Kurds and Shiites were being driven into the rugged mountains bordering Turkey, where they could be vividly witnessed by television.

The vast panorama of suffering, and perhaps even more the individual portraits of agony, seemed overwhelming. Not easily forgotten were scenes like that of the little girl, her bare feet sinking into the freezing mud, or of the little boy, his face burned, possibly by napalm. The anguished face of a child peered up from the cover of *Newsweek*, with the caption, addressed to Mr. Bush, "Why won't he help us?"[7] In a BBC report on *The MacNeil/Lehrer Newshour*, a woman asked, "Why did George Bush do nothing?"

The quagmire-shunning Bush Administration was slow to react, concentrating on a formal cease-fire to speed the return of American troops and continuing to emphasize its refusal to be involved in "an internal conflict."

April 2: On a golf course in Florida, in strange juxtaposition with evening news scenes of shivering and starving refugees, the president brushed off questions about the continued Iraqi use of helicopter gunships against the Kurds, saying, "I feel no reason to answer to anybody. We're relaxing here."

A senior official told the *Washington Post* that the reticence was deliberate: "Engaging on this issue gains us nothing. All you do is risk raising public concerns that are not there now. . . ."[8]

April 3: By now the Administration was becoming aware of American and European "concerns," and had begun scrambling for a

---

5. George Church, *Keeping Hands Off: As Saddam's Loyalists Pound the Rebels, the Carnage Inside Iraq Poses a Quandary with No Attractive Alternatives for the U.S.*, TIME, Apr. 8, 1991, at 22.

6. Tom Matthews et al., *A Quagmire After All*, NEWSWEEK, Apr. 29, 1991, at 23.

7. Ron Moreau, *Saddam's Slaughter*, NEWSWEEK, Apr. 15, 1991, at Cover, 22.

8. Ann Devroy & Al Kamen, *Bush Aides Keep Quiet on Rebels: Defense of Policy Viewed as Risky*, WASH. POST, Apr. 4, 1991, at A2.

policy of compassion without intervention. On the Florida golf course, Mr. Bush said, "I feel frustrated any time innocent civilians are being slaughtered. But the United States and these other countries with us in this coalition did not go there to settle all the internal affairs of Iraq."

Later that day came a written statement in the president's name, departing from the Administration's passive role: "I call upon Iraq's leaders to halt these attacks immediately and to allow international organizations to work inside Iraq to alleviate the suffering. . . . The United States is prepared to extend economic help to Turkey through multilateral channels."

April 4: Appearing with Japanese Prime Minister Toshiki Kaifu in Newport Beach, California, Mr. Bush said, "we will do what we can to help the Kurdish refugees." But he also stuck with the position that no American parent "wants to see the United States forces pushed into this situation, brutal, tough, and deplorable as it is."

By this time, the Kurdish insurrection all but crushed, television was showing a mass exodus into the mountains. A widely distributed Associated Press photo showed a ten-year-old girl in a hospital in northern Iraq being comforted by her mother. The child had lost a hand and an eye in an Iraqi helicopter attack.

April 5: In Newport Beach, a dogged President Bush declared, "we will do what we can to help there without being bogged down into a ground-force action in Iraq." Again, the press office, hours later, came up with a written new policy—the Air Force would start dropping food, blankets, and clothing to Kurdish refugees in northern Iraq.

As a public-television answer, the air drops did not go over very well. The supplies landed in random places: television showed where some Kurds had been killed by falling bales.

April 8: Europe was looking at television, too, seeing reporting— particularly in Britain—that was often more vivid and comprehensive than American television was showing. At a European Community meeting in Luxembourg, British Prime Minister John Major proposed the creation of a protected "enclave" for the Kurds in northern Iraq. Secretary of State James Baker, visiting Luxembourg, saw on television what Europeans were seeing. Then, at the bidding of President Bush, worried about an impression of American insensitivity to the refugees' plight, Baker proceeded to the Turkish border. The seven minute visit turned into a photo opportunity of a special sort. It focused on scenes of desperate Kurds, one saying, in English, "Please,

Mr. Baker I want to talk to you. You've got to do something to help us."

April 11: A Reuters dispatch from Washington noted, "Searing pictures of suffering Iraqi refugees have clouded America's Gulf War triumph and given President Bush a devilish political problem."[9] Part of his problem was that his vacillation on the Kurdish issue had helped to bring down his approval rating from ninety-two to eighty percent in a *Newsweek* poll (seventy-eight percent in a Gallup poll).[10]

April 12: The Administration announced that American troops would be going back into Iraq as part of a relief operation called, "Provide Comfort." Military encampments would be set up, guarded by coalition forces, eventually to be turned over to the United Nations. The announcement came so suddenly as to catch off base Defense Secretary Richard Cheney who, an hour before, had told a news conference that there had been no decision to "actually put forces on the ground in Iraq."

Within a two-week period, the president had been forced, under the impact of what Americans and Europeans were seeing on television, to reconsider his hasty withdrawal of troops from Iraq. As though to acknowledge this, Mr. Bush told a news conference on April 16, "No one can see the pictures or hear the accounts of this human suffering—men, women, and, most painfully of all, innocent children— and not be deeply moved."

Military victory over Iraq was threatening to run into political and moral defeat. The polls that had shown Americans overwhelmingly wanting troops to come home in a hurry were now showing that Americans did not want to abandon the Kurds, even if that meant using American forces to protect them.

It is rare in American history that television, which is most often manipulated to support a policy, creates an unofficial plebiscite that forces a change in policy.

In a column on May 5, *New York Times* television critic Walter Goodman underscored what the medium had wrought when "it compelled the White House to act despite its initial reluctance."[11] But he also raised the question, "Should American policy be driven by

---

9. Gene Gibbons, *Iraq Refugee Plight Creates Political Dilemma for Bush*, Apr. 11, 1991.

10. *Newsweek Poll: Attitudes on Iraq Win Keep Slipping*, NEWSWEEK, Apr. 22, 1991, at Poll Update (reporting poll results from both the *Newsweek* and the Gallup polls).

11. Walter Goodman, *The Images That Haunt Washington*, N.Y. TIMES, May 5, 1991, at B33.

scenes that happen to be accessible to cameras and that make the most impact on the screen?"[12]

The question is a reasonable one. But, in the case of the Kurds, it was not the pictures alone that forced the change. These were not random pictures of random suffering, but pictures that dramatized the suffering of a people for whom Americans felt some responsibility. It was that combination that overwhelmed governmental passivity.

---

12. *Id.*

A Jew in Journalism†

A Jewish journalist is not the same as a Jew in journalism, and I have been both. For seven years, starting in 1934, I practiced Jewish journalism. Still in college, I worked for a newly-launched venture called the *Jewish Daily Bulletin*. It was the first and only English-language Jewish daily. It was founded on the premise that it would fill a gap for American Jews, increasingly Jewish-conscious with the rise of Hitler, but drifting away from the Yiddish press. In support of the premise, the publisher, Jacob Landau, who headed the Jewish Telegraphic Agency, enlisted financial aid from philanthropists like Felix M. Warburg and Jacob Blaustein.

I started as a "stringer," a part-time reporter paid space rates. (I believe that the word "stringer" derives from the early practice of measuring column inches with a piece of string.) I was possibly the most zealous stringer the *Bulletin* had. I covered Sunday sermons of Rabbis Wise, Stephen and Jonah. I wrote a six-part expose of rackets in Jewish charities. I accepted the risky, but profitable assignment of covering the local Nazis—the German-American Bund—who paraded and rallied in Yorkville and Queens, heiling Hitler and threatening the American Jews. The assignment was profitable because I got a lot of space. Then, as now, the media, including the Jewish media, regarded fear as a circulation builder. The press has a symbiotic relationship with those who threaten and practice violence. The *Bulletin* thrived on Nazi threats, and the Nazis thrived on *Bulletin* clippings to show Goebbels how effective they were. When the Bund started breaking up in factional fights, I was courted by each faction, anxious to have its story told in their unofficial organ.

I piled up so many column inches with the Nazis' help that I was soon earning more than most staff reporters. So, I was appointed to the staff. But the *Bulletin* was a money loser not even the Nazis could save. A transitional daily found no place among second-generation Jews, who generally moved from a Yiddish paper to the *New York Times* or *Daily News*. The last days of the *Bulletin* were rather grim. We formed one of the first units of the Newspaper Guild and conducted one of its first strikes. Our demands were not

†. This speech was originally presented under the same title at the Hillel Jewish Student Center, Michigan State University, Mar. 18, 1997.

151

unreasonable—we wanted the many weeks of back pay we were owed. But the *Bulletin*, having by now lost the confidence of its philanthropist backers, could not meet those demands, and the *Bulletin* folded, having lasted little more than two years.

I transferred to the parent Jewish Telegraph Agency, handling cables from bureaus abroad. Our report was furnished by wire to the Associated Press, United Press, and the *New York Times*. I received a liberal education in Cablese, the arcane language of Latin prefixes and word combinations intended to save cable costs. A person arrived *"expoland sinebaggage"* and left *"proamerica."* That was when "play down" first became "downplay," now a part of the American language. A reprimand to a correspondent who overfiled read *"prochrisakes offlay"* (two words).

In this prewar period of a rising Nazi menace in Europe, the JTA carried reports from refugees and other secondary sources telling of persecution and worse. Little of our copy, other than obituaries, was used by the wire services and the *Times*. They suspected that it was propagandistic, and were encouraged so to believe by the State Department. It was interesting to work side by side with the Yiddish desk, rewriting the same incoming cables, making banner headlines in the Yiddish papers, making a negligible impression on the general press.

My work also involved service by mail to the Anglo-Jewish weekly press, whose appetite was as great as our resources were small. So, I wrote under several bylines. Under my own name, serious matters like the retirement of Justice Louis Brandeis or philosopher Morris Raphael Cohen. And, in 1939, an extensive series on "the War and the Jews." As Alvin Hellman, I reviewed theater and music, always concentrating, of course, on the "Jewish angle," which meant favoring Bruno Walter over Leopold Stokowski. As Harry Davis, I wrote a gossip column. A typical item: Rabbi Stephen S. Wise, eating in his favorite Hungarian restaurant, stopped by his wife from eating strudel because it was too fattening. After seven years, the constant quest of the Jewish angle—was Columbus a Jew? Was heavyweight boxer Max Baer really Jewish?—came to weigh on me. But what weighed on me much more was having to view a world plunging into war through the confining prism of Jewish persecution and Jewish tragedy. So, in 1941, expecting to be drafted anyway, I left JTA and Jewish journalism, hoping that after the war I could become a foreign correspondent, perhaps even for the *New York Times*—my great dream.

After the war, I did go to Europe, a stringer again, but now for "general" newspapers—the *Christian Science Monitor, Time* magazine, the *London Daily Mail*, and eventually, the *New York Times*. I lived in The Hague and reported on the Benelux countries. I made the necessary separation between private Jewishness and public neutrality. I could write with detachment about the wartime experiences of the Jews in Holland. I could even-handedly cover negotiations for German reparations to Israel and diaspora Jews. But I reacted with a special fury when my friend, the Israeli minister in The Hague, initially misled me and the *New York Times* about the location of these negotiations. His aim was to thwart possible Arab terrorists. He thought that I, being Jewish, would understand his using me that way. I never forgave him.

I worked hard at being a "general" journalist, general enough to meet the standards of the *Times*. And, in 1952, by now getting many bylines in the *Times*, I flew to New York to tell Turner Catledge, the Managing Editor, that it was time he appointed me to the staff. He said that was a possibility, but he wanted first to test my versatility by having me work for three days on local stories under the city desk. On the third day I broke the story of the plan to build what is now Lincoln Center. Catledge said I had passed the test and should return to Holland, expecting appointment to the staff soon.

Summer and Fall came and went without anything happening. On February 1, 1953, Holland was struck by a deadly combination of storm and high tides that broke the dikes and flooded a large part of the country. I covered that story for the *Times*, and also for CBS with on-the-scene radio reports that attracted the attention of Edward R. Murrow. Out of the blue I received a cable, "Would you at all consider joining the staff of CBS News with an initial assignment in Washington?" Flattering, but I wanted to work for the *Times*. To prod Catledge, I cabled him that I had an offer I would have to consider unless he could promise early action. To my astonishment he replied that I would be well advised to accept the other offer. And so my career shifted abruptly from my long-cherished goal of being a *Times* correspondent to what then seemed a dubious venture into electronic journalism, which has been my main occupation ever since 1953.

An amazing turn of events, but at least no "Jewish angle."

Well, not quite. Having served as CBS diplomatic correspondent and having opened the CBS bureau in Moscow, I returned to New York for year-end programs in 1955. During a social gathering, the *Times* Foreign Editor, Emanuel Freedman, complimented me on my work for CBS, and I replied that, were it not for his paper's foot-dragging I would have been doing it for the *Times*. Next day Freedman invited me to his home for dinner and there, joined by Assistant Managing Editor Ted Bernstein, he told me they had a painful confession to make. It was that just as I was to be named to the staff, Catledge made a policy decision to freeze the hiring of Jews as correspondents. The purported reason was that a disproportionate number of Jews would leave the paper without enough flexibility to cover the Arab side of a Middle East War. The publisher, Arthur Hays Sulzberger, had approved the policy, and, Freedman said, to their shame, he and Bernstein had concurred in it. It was soon rescinded, too late for me. Embarrassing though it was, Manny said, they felt they owed me this explanation of why the *Times*, having promised to hire me, hadn't. Years later the *Times* offered me the position of Diplomatic Correspondent, and so great was the tug of long attachment, that I considered it. But in the end we agreed amicably that my career and life had gone too far on another course to turn the calendar back a quarter century.

So I became a Jew in broadcasting, always patrolling the line between Jewish heritage and journalistic detachment. As an American reporter, I went to the Moscow synagogue to report on availability of matzoh for Passover. In my private capacity, I attended seder in the Israeli embassy and donned a yarmulke. My colleague and friend, Max Frankel of the *New York Times*, and I toured outside Moscow where the authorities would let us. In Kiev, on a Spring morning in 1957, we saw four old Jews sitting on a park bench. We did not approach them—that might have caused difficulty for them with the secret police we assumed were watching us—but we walked back and forth past them, giving them the opportunity to address us if they chose to. Finally, on one of our passes, one of them spoke up, "*Ir zeit Yidden?*" And then we had a conversation in my rusty Yiddish and Max's fluent German during which one of them asked if I knew a relative of his in Philadelphia, and another asked, "Tell me, in America Jews are freely allowed to leave the country?" Max and I did not quote that in our reports on our trip. It would probably not have cleared censorship, and it might have gotten the Jews into trouble for a provocative reference to the ban on Jewish emigration from the Soviet Union.

So, where was my journalistic detachment, my rigorous insistence on keeping my Jewish heritage carefully sequestered from reporting all the news? Where was it? I don't know! In Riga, we were also sensitive to not compromising dissident Latvians we met. Don't think it's only

Jews I worry about. I am not a Jewish Journalist, just a journalist who happens to be Jewish. I have told myself that for almost forty years.

But, yes, then there was the episode in Poland in 1957 when I was working on a documentary for Ed Murrow's *See It Now* series. In a town near the Soviet border I came upon a caravan of horsedrawn carts, piled high with the possessions of Jews on their way to the railway station. On camera, in Yiddish, they told me they were going to Israel. When I asked the Israeli Minister in Warsaw how this was possible, he told me of a delicate secret arrangement permitting Jews in Polish areas annexed by the Soviet Union to be "repatriated" and proceed to Israel. But, the Minister said that because of Arab reaction, the arrangement would be canceled if it became publicly known. And the Israeli diplomat asked if I wanted to be responsible for trapping several thousand Jews in the Soviet Union.

I held onto that film for a long time, never quite deciding to suppress it, but effectively doing so. Would I have killed a good story to save some Kurds, some Armenians, some Slovaks? Maybe. How do I know?

As tough as any assignment for a Jew in journalism is covering Germany, as I did for CBS from 1960 until 1966. Germans are, on the whole, personally speaking, not my favorite people, and that would probably be true even without the Nazi past. I don't instinctively take to them the way I do to the Dutch or the Italians. Yet, when CBS asked me in 1960 whether I would have any problem being assigned, to Bonn, I said that I was fully able to report professionally from anywhere and keep my personal feelings well separated from my work. And, I think that on the whole, I succeeded. I could, without retching, interview Admiral Karl Doenitz, Hitler's successor and last head of the Third Reich, as he told me America had made a mistake fighting Germany and should have been fighting the Russians instead. I could interview the most disgusting German I ever met, communist boss Walther Ulbricht, behind his Wall in 1961, claiming that only West Germans had any responsibility for Hitler. In the end it was he, not I, who interrupted the interview and stormed out of his office in full view of our camera.

I had many German acquaintances and professional associates, and even a few good friends. It helped to observe a new generation of Germans, anxious to face and overcome the past and to be good Europeans. I came to see Germany as a pillar of stability in Europe, and, ironically, even a haven for some Jews from the East.

When a delegation of American Jewish organizations came to Bonn in 1962, after a rash of synagogue and cemetery desecrations around Cologne, one of them, skeptical that a Jew could function as a correspondent in Germany, asked me how widespread I thought anti-Semitism was. I'm afraid I upset her when I said, "Well, there is some, probably not quite as much as in America."

After my return to Washington in 1966, word came that I was to be awarded a German presidential decoration, the Cross of Merit. The woman I was courting, a refugee from Germany, did not take well to the idea. I indicated to the German embassy that I was reluctant to accept the honor. That was apparently interpreted as my playing hard to get, with the result that I was awarded the Grand Cross of Merit. To have rejected it would have been taken as a slap in the face from an American Jew. I decided to accept it. I am happy to report that the lady married me anyway.

At eighty I no longer worry so much about preserving pristine detachment. Although regarded by some as soft on Germany, I have no trouble commenting forcefully on growing xenophobia in Germany and the bleak opportunism of Chancellor Kohl's lunching with Austrian President Waldheim and rebuking the Jews who criticized him. I am comfortable commenting on Arab-Israeli issues, reproved about as much by one side as the other.

As I look back, I am less concerned about a possible conflict of interest or a difference between Jewish Journalist and Jew in journalism. A professional is the sum of many things, and in my case, being Jewish is one of them. To be a journalist, one need not be less a Jew. And, being a Jew, I hope I have been no less a journalist.

The First Amendment Under Pressure†

The last time I spoke at a school in the Bay Area was in 1977 at Berkeley. I was a Regents Professor in Berkeley's Journalism School, a refugee from the CIA, CBS, and Congress back East. My subject was "Limits on Freedom of the Press," and I argued, with some passion, that there shouldn't be many. My views were colored by what I had recently been through on the First Amendment war front.

I had been summoned before the House Ethics Committee in public session and required to name the source from which I had obtained the draft of a report of the House Intelligence Committee on CIA and FBI malfeasances, a report that the House had voted to suppress. If I did not comply, I was warned, I would be subject to being cited for contempt of Congress. That carried the penalty of a stiff prison sentence and a fine. The Supreme Court had ruled, in *Branzburg v. Hayes*, that the First Amendment afforded no absolute protection for a journalist's sources,[1] and so the prospect of jail, as my lawyer, Joseph Califano, explained to me, was very real.

The hearing was being carried live on public television, and it must have elicited some response around the country. At the end of the day, the Committee retired into executive session and voted 6 to 5 against holding me in contempt. Considering the initial hostility of most of the members, condemning me for arrogant disregard for the will of Congress, the Committee's hand may well have been stayed, in the end, by a word from constituents, expressing support for a beleaguered reporter's First Amendment defense.

I am not sure that the public today would rally that way behind a reporter defending a First Amendment right, or "privilege," as it is called in the law. "Privilege" is an interesting word. In its first dictionary meaning: a special advantage, like "the privileges of the very rich;" then, legal immunities for officials, like the President's "executive privilege;" finally, citizen immunities, like lawyer-client privilege, doctor-patient privilege, priest-penitent privilege, and the Fifth Amendment privilege against self-incrimination. And how about

---

† This speech was originally published as the 1996 Mathew O. Tobriner Memorial Lecture in the *Hastings Communications and Entertainment Law Journal*, at 18 HASTINGS COMM/ENT L.J. 433 (1996).

1. Branzburg v. Hayes, 408 U.S. 665, 708-09 (1972).

First Amendment reporter-source privilege? That is less securely anchored in law and in popular acceptance.

Ultimately, privilege must depend on public support, and support for press privilege has ebbed in these twenty years. In part, this is because the First Amendment has been stretched to cover a variety of activities that do not enjoy public approval. We have recently witnessed campaigns against violence and pornography on television, against gangsta rap records, and against exploitative talk shows. All of these enjoy First Amendment protection, but stretching the First Amendment to shield activities regarded as antisocial only weakens support for the First Amendment. I can remember Jules Feiffer, at a conference of the American Civil Liberties Union, being asked how the ACLU could defend *Hustler* magazine.[2] He said, "In the civil liberties business we sometimes have to defend people we wouldn't have dinner with."[3]

By the age of eighteen, according to the National Coalition on Television Violence, the average American will have seen 200,000 acts of violence, including 40,000 murders.[4] All protected by the First Amendment. According to *USA Today*, of forty-five sex scenes counted in a sample television week, only four involved married couples; thirty-nine involved adulterers or unmarried persons.[5] And in none was there indication of anyone using condoms. (For some things First Amendment protection isn't sufficient.)

At my advanced age, I can remember a more innocent age on television. In 1950, the words "hell" and "damn" were first used on the CBS Arthur Godfrey show.[6] In 1961, Yvette Mimieux showed the first woman's navel on a Dr. Kildare episode.[7] Television has come a long way since, baby. But now television is on a collision course not only with those concerned about religious values, but those more generally concerned about children and about the level of taste in America.

I wish I could encapsulate the journalism part of the information-entertainment-infotainment spectrum and say, "This, at least, deserves

---

2. Jules Feiffer, Conference of the American Civil Liberties Union.

3. *Id.*

4. Christopher Lee Philips, *Task Force on TV Violence*, BROADCASTING & CABLE, June 14, 1993, at 69.

5. Barbara Hansen & Carol Knopes, *TV vs. Reality*, USA TODAY, July 6, 1993, at 1A.

6. Sheila Muto, *Television: From Here to Immodesty: Milestones in the Toppling of TV's Taboos*, WALL ST. J., Sept. 15, 1995, at B1.

7. *Id.*

the public's full support." But journalism no longer exists in isolation. The "press" has become absorbed into "the news media," which, in turn are being absorbed into mega-media conglomerates. Will ABC investigate Disney? Will Fox investigate Murdoch and Gingrich?

Look at this example of potential conflict of interest. Today at the annual meeting of the American Public Health Association in San Diego, medical researchers of the University of California, San Francisco are reporting on what happened to the popular school children's weekly, the *Weekly Reader*, after it was bought by a subsidiary of RJR Nabisco, maker of Camel cigarettes.[8] Whereas the *Weekly*'s tobacco-related articles previously presented a consistently anti-smoking message, now the "presentation of the issue was significantly more consonant with the messages the industry likes to send."[9] And Joe Camel made frequent appearances, in one case in a full-page color cover picture.[10] The First Amendment protects that, too.

What has happened, meanwhile, to the public perception of the journalist? The image of the underpaid reporter with the press card in his greasy hatband is pretty well gone, and the newspaper he worked for is going. The news media figure today is a blow-dried million-dollar anchor person, more celebrated than the celebrities he or she covers.

The news program, occupying a little corner of a vast entertainment stage, is forced to compete with *Hard Copy* and other versions of reality that are not reality. So, NBC rigged a GM truck to explode, and ABC used actors to simulate an alleged American spy handing a briefcase full of secrets to a KGB agent.[11] And, for a thankfully short period several years ago, CBS News employed a casting director for a "news" magazine program.

Inside the industry there is some agonizing and soul-searching. Before the Radio-Television News Directors Association a few weeks ago, Andrew Lack, President of NBC News, talked of all the cops kicking down crackhouse doors and the victims sobbing about sexual molestation that have become the stuff of television news, and said, "We are, as a profession, going downhill in certain major respects."[12]

---

8. Laura Beil, *Picking the Habit*, DALLAS MORNING NEWS, Nov. 20, 1995, at 6D.

9. *Id.*

10. *Id.*

11. Carleton R. Bryant, *Staging the News*, WASH. TIMES, Feb. 10, 1993, at A3.

12. Andrew Lack, *TV News Heads Downhill*, USA TODAY, Sept. 14, 1995, at 11A; Steve McClellan, *Lack Lays into TV News: In RTNDA Keynote, NBC President Says Profession Helping 'Dumb Down' America*, BROADCASTING & CABLE, Sept. 11, 1995, at

All of this has the effect of putting a strain on the First Amendment because it erodes public support for what the journalist does. The fact is that the public tends to view the news media today as arrogant, insensitive, and self-serving—as self-serving as the institutions the press professes to monitor. Big Media is as unpopular as Big Government.

There are other strains. The tobacco industry clings to the sagging First Amendment much as the gun-slingers and pornographers do. The cigarette people invoke the First Amendment in court to resist regulations aimed at protecting children from the dangers of smoking. The First Amendment is not absolute. Commercial speech does not enjoy the same protection as political speech, or even the same protection as sex and violence.[13] You are not free to label food and drugs falsely, not free to misrepresent securities, nor to advertise the sale of heroin.[14]

Recently, the Supreme Court heard a case involving the claim that Rhode Island's ban on advertising liquor prices violates free speech.[15] A dozen or so other states have similar bans, which are obviously intended to reduce alcohol consumption.[16] The American Civil Liberties Union has joined conservative legal foundations to support the liquor industry. I understand why the ACLU feels it must defend the First Amendment in its most absolute and dissolute terms, but I wish it would concentrate on ordinary pornography, rather than the obscenity of using the First Amendment for profit at the expense of the public health.

My primary concern is that public support for the First Amendment, already at a low ebb, not be further weakened by the appearance of being invoked unreasonably. In the O.J. Simpson trial, the defense, at one point, considered calling as a witness Tracy Savage of television station KNBC.[17] She had reported that DNA tests

---

16.

13. See, e.g., Central Hudson Gas & Elec. Corp. v. Public Service Comm'n of New York, 447 U.S. 557 (1980) (setting the standard for protection of commercial speech as a four part test including whether or not the government interest is a substantial one).

14. See, e.g., id.; Friedman v. Rogers, 440 U.S. 1 (1979).

15. See 44 Liquormart, Inc. v. Rhode Island, 517 U.S. 484 (1996).

16. See ORC Ann. 4301.03 (Anderson 1995); M. David LeBrun, Annotation, *Validity, Construction, and Effect of Statutes, Ordinances, or Regulations Prohibiting or Regulating Advertising of Intoxicating Liquors*, 20 ALR 4th 600 (1995).

17. William Carlsen, *Defense Won't Be Allowed to See Leak Files*, S.F. CHRON., Aug. 10, 1995, at A8.

showed that blood on a sock was that of Simpson's ex-wife.[18] Presumably she would have invoked the First Amendment and refused to identify her source. But it couldn't have been much of a source because the story was wrong; the DNA test had not even been run yet.[19]

That leads me to the question of televising trials. Having, over the years, been involved in numerous arguments about access for radio and television (the camera and the microphone are to us what the pencil is to the print reporter), I must theoretically hold that television should be admitted to all courtrooms. But, in my declining years, I am no longer a believer in absolutes. Clearly, the camera encourages lawyers and witnesses to grandstand. It promotes an industry of exploitation of media "celebrityhood." It can, in case of a mistrial, complicate the task of selecting a second jury. So, I will not argue too vehemently with any judge who decides to limit television access to his or her courtroom.

We have not recently had the kind of dramatic press freedom confrontation that makes the public appreciate the importance of this privilege. It was not very helpful to the cause that an editor in St. Paul, Minnesota, violated a reporter's promise to safeguard the identity of a confidential source, with the result that the source sued for breach of contract.[20]

The most interesting press freedom case recently has been the gag order imposed on *Business Week* by Federal Judge John Feikens in Cincinnati preventing the magazine from publishing court documents under seal which it had managed to obtain.[21] This was clearly an egregious example of prior restraint, although not on the level of the Pentagon Papers.[22]

I am nostalgic for the Pentagon Papers case, which had everything I would want to see in a First Amendment case. Here was the Nixon Administration seeking to enjoin the publication of Vietnam history on the ground that it would irreparably harm the national security of the United States.[23] Yet the government was totally unable to

---

18. *Id.*

19. *Id.*

20. *See* Ruzicka v. Conde Nast Publications, Inc., 999 F.2d 1319 (8th Cir. 1993).

21. Proctor & Gamble v. Bankers Trust Co., 900 F. Supp. 186 (S.D. Ohio 1995), *vacated*, 1196 U.S. App. LEXIS 3817 (6th Cir. Ohio Mar. 5, 1996). *See also* Linda Himelstein, *The Story Behind the Bankers Trust Story*, BUS. WK., Oct 2, 1995, at 58.

22. *See* New York Times, Co. v. United States, 403 U.S. 713 (1971) (per curiam).

23. *See id.*

demonstrate harm to the satisfaction of a federal judge.[24] That case, argued by the *New York Times* and *Washington Post* after they had submitted to prior restraint, is what you call striking a real blow for freedom of the press.[25] It served the public and exploded an official lie. It showed that, on the whole, the public interest suffers more from excessive secrecy than from excessive disclosure. Chalk up one for the First Amendment.

But, given the contemporary situation, how does a press, whose motive and dedication to the public weal are suspect, go about restoring public support for our "privilege?" How do we overcome the public attitude that evidenced itself when the press protested against censorship in the Gulf war and opinion polls indicated the public favored more censorship?

The case of the Unabomber and the publication of his creed in the *Washington Post* may suggest one approach we may have to adopt.[26] The Unabomber, demanding publication of his 32,000-word paper as the price for desisting from further murders, gave a new meaning to "publish or perish."[27] And the *Post*, submitting to the demand, gave a new meaning to "publish and be damned."[28] For there were a great many who damned the *Post* and the *New York Times* for submitting to "blackmail," thus possibly inviting copy-catting.

I support the decision of the papers. As a matter of restoring a link with the public, the press must do something to overcome the prevailing impression of arrogance and insensitivity to the concerns of ordinary people. I thought the *Times* publisher, Arthur Sulzburger, had it right when he said that this issue "centers on the role of a newspaper as part of a community."[29] In a community, faced with the choice between principle and life, you may have to choose life.

Let's face it. They don't like us newspeople out there any more. They think we manipulate and exploit them for fun and profit. They are no longer willing to forgive us our press passes. I am not so utopian as to hope that the media mega-corporations will forswear profit and rededicate themselves to the public interest. But whatever we can do

---

24.   *Id.*

25.   *Id.*

26.   *Industrial Society and Its Future*, WASH. POST, Sept. 19, 1995, at A1.

27.   Daniel Schorr, *Publishing the Unabomber: Responsible or Reckless? Printing Was a Tough But Conscionable Choice*, WASH. POST, Sept. 24, 1995, at C3.

28.   *Id.*

29.   William Serrin, *The Papers Submitted to Blackmail by a Killer*, WASH. POST, Sept. 24, 1995, at C3.

to convince the public that their interest means something to us will serve the First Amendment.

One possible new direction has been outlined by my friend, Ellen Hume, in a study for the Annenberg Washington Program of Northwestern University on the impact of technology on journalism. She finds that "the apparently endless flow of scandals and feeding frenzies has damaged rather than enhanced journalism's credibility."[30] The objective now, she says, must be to use new technologies to create "a trustworthy product."[31] Addressing a "public" rather than an "audience."

The smart new journalism will be both interactive and proactive, opening the door for citizen engagement. In the new news marketplace, Ellen sees an end to the obsession with scoops and deadlines.

I may be too old to grasp what lies ahead in a new interactive journalism geared to a new technological age. I can only surmise that anything that helps to restore public confidence in the disseminators of information will help to restore public support for the constitutional guarantee of the freedom of the press. The men who crafted that guarantee to shield the writers of political polemics from retaliation by Congress could not have dreamed what a vast industry their brief amendment would end up shielding. But it is still, perhaps more than ever, worth fighting to protect.

---

30. Richard Harwood, *Extinct Stained Wretches?*, WASH. POST, Nov. 2, 1995, at A31.
31. *Id.*